Also from the Author

You can develop the skills to meet the needs of learners in any learning environment.

This approachable, in-depth guide unites the adaptability of Universal Design for Learning with the flexibility of blended learning, equipping educators with the tools they need to create relevant, authentic, and meaningful learning pathways to meet students where they're at, no matter the time and place or their pace and path. With step-by-step guidance and clear strategies, authors Katie Novak and Catlin Tucker empower teachers to implement these frameworks in the classroom, with a focus on cultivating community, building equity, and increasing accessibility for all learners.

As we face increasing uncertainty and frequent disruption to traditional ways of living and learning, *UDL and Blended Learning* offers bold, innovative, inclusive solutions for navigating a range of learning landscapes, from the home to the classroom and all points in between, no matter what obstacles may lie ahead.

Catlin Tucker and Katie Novak have worked with too many educators who are frustrated and disillusioned with the teaching profession. They know that teachers are drowning in work and unrealistic demands. Many are mentally and emotionally exhausted by the uncertainty and constant change. In this follow-up to *UDL and Blended Learning*, the authors have set out to help teachers reimagine their approach to this work so that it is sustainable and rewarding.

Each chapter in *The Shift to Student-Led* takes apart one traditional teacher-led workflow, examining the problems it presents teachers and students, what the research says versus what the reality in the classroom is, and how UDL and blended learning can free teachers from the "sage on the stage" role and place students at the center of their learning. These reimagined student-led workflows help students develop self-awareness, internal motivation, and self-regulation skills, which are critical to becoming expert learners.

Intended for K–12 educators, instructional coaches, and school leaders who want to create academically robust, inclusive learning communities, this book is full of principles, strategies, and resources that can be put into practice right away and at any level.

This book is an essential resource for all educators. To address declining literacy skills, every educator needs to become a teacher of writing. In every grade and subject, the writing process enables students to interpret complex ideas, cultivate their individual voices, and shape and share their learning.

As writing becomes more efficient with the aid of AI chatbots, there's an unparalleled opportunity for educators across all content areas to reimagine their approach to writing. In *Shift Writing into the Classroom*, UDL and blended learning experts Catlin R. Tucker and Katie Novak invite educators to focus on human connection, sitting alongside learners to understand their specific needs and provide individualized instruction and support across *all* grades and content areas. Tucker and Novak transform traditional writing workflows to provide students with meaningful opportunities in the classroom to work through the writing process, collaborate with peers, and produce original writing that addresses task, purpose, and audience creatively and authentically.

Ideal for schools and districts prioritizing the integration of literacy across the curriculum, this book offers practical guidance, strategies, and resources to elevate students' writing abilities in every subject.

Educators understand the crucial importance of developing learning experiences that are accessible, engaging, and student-centered. However, when faced with a long list of ever-increasing demands, teachers are often left without the time, energy, and resources necessary to turn best intentions into best practices. Enter *Elevating Educational Design with AI*, a guide for teachers who want to use technology to activate engagement, give students agency over their learning, and streamline workflows.

In an era when AI is rapidly reshaping our world, some educators feel apprehensive about integrating it into their practice. Without a focus on the humans behind the ideas, AI-generated lessons can end up perpetuating one-size-fits-all learning experiences, undermining efforts to create inclusive and differentiated learning environments where all students can thrive. The conversational, personable, and inquisitive approach of *Elevating Educational Design with AI* refocuses the conversation on how we can use AI-powered tools in the service of strong pedagogical practices that offer effective learning experiences for every student, demystifying the integration of AI in education, guiding educators, and helping them harness its power.

The UDL Shift

KATIE NOVAK

THE UDL *Shift*

Designing
Inclusive Learning
THAT WORKS

The UDL Shift: Designing Inclusive Learning That Works

Published by IMPress, a division of Dave Burgess Consulting, Inc.
IMPressbooks.org
DaveBurgessConsulting.com
Vancouver, WA

Library of Congress Control Number: 2026936825
Paperback ISBN: 978-1-948334-85-3
Ebook ISBN: 978-1-948334-86-0

Cover and interior design by Liz Schreiter
Edited and produced by Reading List Editorial
ReadingListEditorial.com

As a mom of four, I am constantly in awe of the teachers who go above and beyond to teach, inspire, connect, and create meaningful memories for my children. Your care, commitment, and belief in children shape not only their learning but who they become. Thank you, truly, for being part of my village.

Contents

Tables and Figures

INTRODUCTION

For the Love of Educators

For as long as I can remember, I wanted to be a writer. As a kid in elementary and middle school, I dreamed of creating a bestselling series like *The Baby-Sitters Club* or *Sweet Valley Twins*. By high school, I fancied myself the next great romance novelist of my generation. Recently, while cleaning out some old boxes, I came across a notebook filled with my teenage short stories and poems. I laughed out loud, cringed, and quickly tucked them back in the box.

While my storytelling has thankfully evolved since those early drafts, the potential of a blank page, the hope that someone might find meaning in my words, and my passion for writing have never faded. I may not be holed up in a fabulous beach cottage writing the next great novel, but I found that same spark in another space: the classroom. My love for writing is one of the reasons I became an English teacher, and some of my best memories are from those years spent teaching high school or middle school English, surrounded by hilarious, big-hearted colleagues.

We all have those stories:

- Remember when Pete's boa constrictor, Petunia, escaped during winter break and was at large in the building?

- How about when our student Jamie told us, point-blank in a team meeting, that the reason he wasn't excelling was because every one of us was "painfully boring"? (Spoiler: He wasn't completely wrong. I asked the class to weigh in, and they confirmed I could be "cool, fun, and occasionally boring." So we redesigned the class together.)

My years in the classroom weren't just full of amazing stories. They shaped my understanding of what educators truly need: community, creativity, and space to try, fail, and try again. They also highlighted the challenges that, with thoughtful and intentional design, could be transformed if we were willing to be creative and flexible, thinking out of the box.

You see, our stories aren't just memorable and hilarious. In those moments, we faced a real barrier, and we innovated. That's what educators do, especially when we're trusted to do it well. Whether we're luring out a snake with heating pads before the principal finds out Petunia is missing or co-designing a feedback system with middle schoolers, we rise to the occasion when we're given space to think differently.

We rise to the occasion when we're given space to think differently.

I honestly thought I'd spend my entire career in the classroom, but as I began teaching graduate courses, I discovered something: I loved working with educators just as much as I loved teaching kids. We're a fabulous bunch, and this book is for all of us—teachers, coaches, specialists, service providers, and leaders—who want to make teaching more efficient, more inclusive, and even more joyful. Goodness knows we could all use a little more joy in our lives.

This is my seventeenth book, and while it builds on ideas I first explored in the three versions of *UDL Now!*, it's not a new edition. It's a whole new book. The educational landscape has changed: Student populations are more diverse, cognitive science is rapidly evolving, and technology (including artificial intelligence) is transforming how we design and deliver instruction. So, it was time to bring together everything I've learned in nearly twenty-five years of education in the hope that it may help you take the next step in this beautiful adventure of teaching and learning.

Where We're Headed

This book is a journey from mindset to methodology. It is organized to help you better understand how to create an environment that is designed with intention to help all learners, regardless of their needs, work toward the same rigorous standards and build the skills that will help them to excel in the future paths they choose. The book has four parts, and every part aims to provide practical strategies to support you in your role:

- In part 1, we'll surface the three Universal Design for Learning (UDL) tenets—variability is the rule, firm goals are met with flexible means, and learner agency is essential—and show why one-size-fits-all instruction doesn't meet the needs of all learners.
- In part 2, we'll make the planning process concrete. Using the UDL Guidelines and a UDL Planning Protocol, you'll better understand how to set firm goals, design flexible pathways, and build agency into daily routines, improving the outcomes for learners and creating more balance for yourself.
- In part 3, we'll take on the bigger systems, including how to adapt adopted curriculum, prepare students for high-stakes

assessments without narrowing learning, and influence systems to better support classroom practice.
- And in part 4 (which is short and sweet!), we'll bring it all together with a fleshed-out UDL Planning Protocol so you feel ready to transform your classroom, one-on-one sessions with students, or faculty meetings.

To help you put ideas into action, the QR code to the left links to practical tools and templates referenced throughout the book. These include planning protocols, sample lessons, reflection guides, and classroom-ready supports you can adapt to your context. As you read, you can scan the QR code to access those materials, organized by chapter.

In every chapter, you'll find my own stories, design shifts, reflection questions, and practical strategies that work for teachers, service providers, and school leaders alike. This isn't just a book about teaching students with individualized education programs (IEPs) or multilingual learners; it is about educating all students in ways that honor their strengths, support their areas of challenge, and prepare them to succeed in the future.

Whether you're reading this over lunch, during your prep period, or from the sidelines at soccer practice, I hope each chapter feels like a conversation with a colleague who respects your time, your brilliance, and your commitment to students. Some of you may already be familiar with UDL and are looking for new ideas to inspire you. If you're new to UDL, welcome to a design framework that will change the way you think about nearly everything. And if you're like me, you're already deeply committed to UDL and recognize that learning is an ongoing journey, one fueled by reflection, research, and now, artificial intelligence (oh my!). There are always new things to learn, and I'm thrilled to share what I've discovered with you. Regardless of where you are in your journey, my hope is that you'll find enough new ideas here to feel affirmed, refreshed, and challenged to take the next step in your UDL practice.

Making the Shift: Who Are You Designing for and With?

Before diving into chapter 1, take a moment to think about the learners at the heart of your school, district, or organization. Think about the kids who are navigating anxiety or trauma, the students who need more of a challenge than the current curriculum provides, and the ones who have been told that grade-level work is not for them.

Now think about the adults: the educators who are doing everything they can to meet student needs, the ones who feel energized when they collaborate and discouraged when they are left to figure it out alone. Think of your colleagues who are hungry for change but are drowning in initiatives labeled "urgent," who feel like maybe improving outcomes for all students is out of reach. These are the people UDL is meant to support. We start by simply thinking about barriers.

For example, a fourth-grade teacher might realize that her highly capable readers aren't getting texts that challenge them. A middle school teacher might notice that the same handful of students never participate in group work, even when significant scaffolds are provided. A district leader might learn from feedback that professional learning sessions are often rated lower by counselors who feel the content isn't as relevant to their work. Noticing these patterns is the first step toward redesign. Because we have to believe that everyone will be successful when we get the conditions right, we look to design when learners aren't experiencing success. And that is what this book is all about.

Up Next

What does it really mean to design with all learners in mind? In chapter 1, we'll explore why one-size-fits-all learning experiences don't work and how UDL offers a better way forward. You'll learn about New England coffee culture and see how designing with flexibility helps more learners succeed. The best part? UDL doesn't just help your learners. It makes your job more inspiring, more manageable, and more rewarding, too.

PART 1

Rewriting the Script

CHAPTER 1

One-Size Doesn't Fit Anyone

"The Regular" Isn't for Everyone

If you ever visit New England and walk into a Dunkin' (or Dunks, as we call it), you'll be likely to overhear someone ordering a "regulah." That's local shorthand for a hot coffee with extra cream and extra sugar. Around here, it's as much a cultural staple as the Red Sox or leaf-peeping in the fall. Some people swear by it, claiming it tastes like coffee ice cream in a cup. Others won't touch it.

One of the best parts of walking into a café is the chance to choose. Just as Dunks offers different ways to enjoy coffee, our learning environments can offer different ways to reach the same learning goal. Whether it's a high school student needing a quiet environment to focus on complex science equations, a kindergartner who benefits from manipulatives and guided practice to stay engaged in early math tasks, or a vocational student who thrives with visual instructions, the principle is the same: Provide varied pathways to meet diverse needs so students can choose what works best.

Too often, schools will argue that they are "already doing" UDL, but honestly, UDL can't be measured in the intentions of the designers. A classroom is only universally designed if *all* students can be included and *all* students have what they need to learn at high levels. We know from the evidence that not all students have opportunities to learn at high levels yet, so by definition, we are still on the journey toward truly universal design. This doesn't mean that schools and teachers are not trying to create more inclusive and flexible learning environments. It just means that we are not there yet, so we must commit to reflection, innovation, and growth.

A classroom is *only* universally designed if all students can be included and all students have what they need to learn at high levels.

I get that shifting to create more flexible classrooms while maintaining rigor may feel overwhelming, but it doesn't have to be. Small shifts in practice, when rooted in UDL, can have a big impact. And sometimes, the most important strategies to start with are the simplest ones. That's where one of my favorite strategies comes in.

The Power of "Would You Rather"

In the spirit of choice, one of my favorite ways to integrate flexibility into learning design is "would you rather." It's simple, requires minimal to no prep, and helps build flexibility into existing lessons. Here's what it might look like:

- In a preschool morning meeting, a teacher might say, "Would you rather sit crisscross applesauce on a carpet square, kneel on a cushion, or bring over your chair? Pick the spot where your body listens best."

- In a reading intervention, an educator might say, "Would you rather read the passage using the screen reader or follow along while I read aloud?"
- In a high school English class, a teacher might say, "Would you rather highlight and annotate in the margins as you read or create a visual summary to identify the main ideas?"
- In a faculty meeting on assessment strategies, a principal might say, "Would you rather brainstorm ideas with your department or contribute your thoughts to a shared online document?"

This strategy isn't just for icebreakers or a quick do-now activity. It's an ongoing way to allow learners to reflect, explore different pathways, name their preferences, and build more autonomy. Over time, they begin to recognize what works for them and why, which builds self-awareness and confidence. You can use this strategy at the start of a lesson, during independent work, or even as part of an exit ticket.

But here's the thing. The cleverness of the strategy is not just the inherent choice; it's that by providing choice, we can eliminate barriers that may exclude some learners by design. Imagine a kindergarten literacy lesson focused on retelling, where students choose between drawing a picture about the story, acting it out, or retelling it to a partner. This eliminates potential linguistic, fine motor, and social-emotional barriers and honors student creativity. A high school science class may offer students the choice between writing a lab report, creating a video explaining the results of an experiment, or designing a presentation for their peers, all of which allow them to communicate the results of a scientific experiment. In a vocational training program, learners could create a written log, photo journal, or video diary to document their progress on a project like building a piece of furniture, wiring a circuit, or preparing a meal. Each of these options supports the same learning goal while honoring individual strengths and preferences and eliminating the potential barriers inherent in one-size-fits-all approaches.

Let's imagine how this looks when it comes together in a classroom. In a fourth-grade science lesson, students are examining ecosystems to build their background knowledge. The teacher partners with the library media specialist, who provides explicit instruction on using various tools to find reliable resources. After exploring their options, some students may find and print a science article, others may listen to a digital version of an article, and a few may curl up in small groups, taking turns reading aloud and pausing to clarify understanding. Other students may access videos or short podcasts and watch or listen while they learn. As they delve into resources, they also choose how to make their thinking visible. Some students may jot notes or respond to questions in a notebook, while others annotate the text or draw visuals that capture the key ideas. And we're just scratching the surface on this. There are so many subtle ways that we can provide our learners with options and choices to build engagement, enhance creativity, and increase learning outcomes while working toward the same firm goals.

"Would you rather" isn't just a classroom strategy. It works across student support roles, too. A couple of meaningful options can increase engagement and make support feel collaborative rather than passive. Here are a few ways it can show up:

- During an SEL check-in, a school counselor might ask, "Would you rather draw how you're feeling or talk it out before we begin our session?"
- A speech-language pathologist assessing fluency could ask, "Would you rather describe this picture or tell me a story?"
- A family liaison might ask parents, "Would you rather get weekly updates by text, email, or a quick video message?"

When providing flexibility using the "would you rather" strategy, all options must align with firm goals. Throughout this book, I will refer to grade-level standards when talking about firm goals, but that term can be easily adapted for use in systems that emphasize curriculum outcomes, competencies, learning goals, or intentions. If you're working in special education, you may be designing instruction specifically aligned with a student's IEP goals. If you are a principal, you support educators as they work toward the goals outlined in the educator evaluation process. Don't get caught up in the language of grade-level standards. The heart of this work is designing inclusive, learner-centered experiences that ensure everyone has what they need to succeed as they work toward goals that are relevant and rigorous—and that matter.

UDL doesn't change what learners are expected to know, nor does it minimize the importance of building academic, behavioral, linguistic, and social-emotional skills. Rather, it changes how they get there. We're not letting go of expectations; we're designing intentionally to make sure more learners can meet them. You'll see how this plays out in more detail with firm goals and flexible means in chapter 5. And let's be honest: When students are more engaged and successful, teaching feels better, too.

Now, to be clear, designing flexible learning experiences is a powerful start, but it's only part of the equation. We'll come back to this later, but for now, just know this: UDL can't carry the full weight of inclusion, nor inclusive practice, alone. We also need systems that support planning, collaboration, and shared responsibility for the educators who serve our students. We will dive into the systems work in chapter 9. All of this is to say that I'm not minimizing the importance of a multi-tiered system of supports (MTSS). That matters. A lot. So if you're a school or district leader, or you're someone who's currently running into barriers that feel bigger than your classroom or role, feel free to jump ahead to chapter 9 and come back. You won't hurt my feelings. (;

If systems are so important, why are we starting with design? It's because this is what every educator can do right now. You don't need a new initiative, a new role, or a new schedule to begin building more flexible, inclusive, student-centered learning experiences. Of course, it will be easier to scale and fully implement if the systems are in place, but you don't have to wait for that. You can begin today.

If systems are so important, why are we starting with design? It's because this is what every educator can do right now. You don't need a new initiative, a new role, or a new schedule to begin building more flexible, inclusive, student-centered learning experiences.

LEADERSHIP LENS

As a leader, your role in UDL implementation is less about mastering every strategy and more about setting the stage for success. That means cultivating a culture where trying new approaches like "would you rather" is encouraged. You'll do this while knowing it takes practice and ongoing feedback to build an environment where both educators and students are comfortable providing and making responsible choices.

I once worked with a principal who carried around little bags of M&M's to give out in celebration of educators trying new things. The candies represented the value of Making Mistakes. (Get it?) When teachers took risks, it was a cause for celebration; even if things didn't work out, they could reflect on why with their students. That small, sweet gesture (pun intended!) sent a big message that innovation was valued.

Consider your own way to celebrate flexibility and risk-taking: Have you made it clear to your staff that you value experimentation over perfection? How?

A school where UDL thrives is one where teachers know their leaders will back them up when they innovate. If you believe that, work to ensure all educators know it's OK to make mistakes as they commit to this work.

Your Move: Turning Insight into Intention

Before moving on, take a breath and check in with yourself. You've just reflected on some big ideas: the limits of one-size-fits-all teaching, the promise of UDL as a framework to better meet the needs of learners (starting with a simple "would you rather"), and the reality that inclusion will require system support. So now what? Try these ideas:

- Analyze where you've already created space for learner choice or flexibility. What made it work? What conditions supported success?
- Design a small shift. Choose one lesson, routine, or system this week and redesign it with more flexibility using "would you rather." What options will you offer? What barriers will those options eliminate? How will you know it worked?
- Envision what success could look like if you were able to fully implement UDL. If every learner had more voice, more flexibility, and more agency (and you experienced more balance and joy), what might change in your classroom or school?

Up Next

Now that we've explored the importance of flexibility, we need to step back and examine our beliefs about learners, our roles in education, and what students need to succeed in the future. So, let's address the critical mindset shifts necessary to embrace the UDL framework and how those shifts will support pedagogical practice.

CHAPTER 2

The Beliefs Behind the Blueprint

From Sprinter to Ultra Runner

I used to think I wasn't built for distance. In high school, I was a sprinter: fast, explosive, and done in a quarter mile or less. The thought of even an eight-hundred-meter race was mind-boggling. The girls on the cross-country team? I was convinced they had lost their minds. One of my best friends, Robyn, once ran home from school—ran—five miles. I was floored. That kind of endurance wasn't in my DNA. Or so I believed.

Fast-forward a few decades, and I've now completed multiple ultramarathons, including a fifty-mile race that pushed me and my poor toes to every edge of my physical and mental limits. I didn't wake up one day and magically become an endurance athlete. It happened slowly, mile by mile, belief by belief. First, a 5K. Then a 10K. Then a half-marathon. With every race, I learned something new: how to fuel (real food only, never Gu, ever), how to pace myself, how to recover (shout-out to hot tubs and Shakti mats), and how to trust my body. I found my groove in my favorite Saucony running shoes and discovered that sometimes the best race-day fuel is a cheeseburger, eaten cold, halfway through the race, with ketchup only and no regrets.

But more than anything, I learned that the limits I believed I had were wrong. They weren't facts. They were stories I had accepted as truth. Just as I had to chip away at my self-imposed limits, we educators need to look closely at the stories we've told ourselves about what students can and can't do—and what we can and can't do ourselves. Belief is not a switch, and it doesn't happen overnight. It's a practice, one that shapes every step of our design process.

The Belt Moment: How Beliefs Show Up in Lesson Plans

In teacher lounges, it's common to hear things like "They're just not ready for grade-level work," "He needs to work on behavior before he can access academics," or "She just doesn't care about school." These comments may come from a place of frustration or concern, but they often reflect deeper assumptions. As educators and leaders, we all carry beliefs about what students can do, who they might become, and what our role is in helping them get there. Sometimes those beliefs push us to innovate and support. Other times, they may quietly limit what we offer and expect.

That's why, before we talk more deeply about strategy, we need to talk about beliefs. Not just what we say we believe but what we actually believe. Whether we realize it or not, our assumptions shape our actions. And those actions shape outcomes.

While UDL is often introduced as a framework for lesson design or differentiated supports, its deepest power lies in how it helps us confront and shift our expectations for learners. Let me take you back to a day in my classroom: The lesson was solid. Objectives were posted. What I had planned was aligned, rigorous, and (I thought) engaging. Everything was humming along until she raised her hand.

While UDL is often introduced as a framework for lesson design or differentiated supports, its deepest power lies in how it helps us confront and shift our expectations for learners.

You have to understand, this student—let's call her Millie—never raised her hand. And if I'm being honest, I had stopped expecting her to. I would have argued that I still held high expectations for the curriculum, but not always for how students would engage with it, especially students like Millie, who had rarely shown interest. So when her hand shot up, I felt a spark. A breakthrough, maybe! A question! A connection! I called on her with genuine excitement.

She looked me dead in the eye and said, "You know, you look way better when you tuck in your shirt and wear a belt."

I blinked. "Do you have a question . . . about the lesson?"

She winked, actually winked. "Nope. Just thought you should know."

I have no memory of what I was teaching that day. But I remember that moment. Not because of the belt (or lack thereof) but because it exposed an assumption I had been holding. I was genuinely surprised that she raised her hand; I had stopped believing she would. That moment reminded me how easy it is to slip into planning *at* students instead of with students in mind. UDL helps pull us back to our *core* beliefs. Consider this belief that may lead us astray:

Belief A: This student needs to be able to sit still and listen to learn effectively. If you believe that quiet compliance is a critical skill, you may design lessons that are built on teacher-directed instruction, expecting all students to take notes quietly at their desks as you explain the content. After the lecture, your plan might include a rigorous task for independent practice. This will likely work for some learners, but in an inclusive classroom, it would create significant barriers for others.

Now, consider the next belief:

Belief B: All students can learn this content, and their variability in engagement and processing is normal and expected. In this scenario, because you embrace flexibility and variability, you proactively build in flexible engagement options. Your lesson plan now includes a short mini-lesson (recorded for later review) followed by a choice of activities: a collaborative discussion, an interactive digital simulation, or a text analysis with a scaffolded graphic organizer. You plan for check-ins with small groups and individuals to monitor progress and provide targeted instruction and action-oriented feedback. In this scenario, more students find ways to engage with the content and demonstrate their understanding through various means. You see engagement and learning rather than just compliance.

When we operate from the belief that variability is expected, not an exception, it changes everything. Flexibility becomes a tool for equity, helping each learner and family access their goals through the means that work best for them. For example, an IEP meeting can be held at school or on Zoom, and it can be supported with interpretation, childcare, and a simple way for families to share input in advance. Families can choose how they receive updates and how they participate in goal-setting so the partnership feels possible and respectful. We honor the variability of the students and families we serve.

That's what UDL helps us do. Not just add tools or tweak tasks but return to our core beliefs. It challenges us to assume capability, even when learners don't show up the way we expect them to. It invites us to see moments of disengagement not as defiance or disinterest but as data telling us something in the design isn't connecting yet. And it reminds us that just because a student or family hasn't yet engaged doesn't mean they won't. Or can't.

It wasn't that I didn't care about my students. I did. Fiercely. But somewhere along the way, I had started bracing for disconnection. I'd plan strong lessons, post clear objectives, and quietly hope for buy-in. I had shifted into coverage mode: delivering content, crossing my fingers, and measuring success by who kept up. I wasn't teaching the students I had. I was teaching the ones I expected to be there.

The moment with the belt is still a core memory for me, as it reminded me that UDL isn't just about choices. It's about actively designing with the belief that all students can engage deeply, think critically, and grow when we create an environment that supports them in doing so. And when we believe that, we plan differently. We teach differently. We show up differently. I mean, to this day, I rock a French tuck every time I wear a shirt long enough to tuck in.

Your lesson plan or the way you design your meetings or professional development sessions reflects your belief system in action. Every choice you make—what you frontload, how you group learners, what options you offer—tells a story about what you believe learners need and who you believe can succeed. So take a moment to ask yourself these questions: Who have I been planning for? Who have I been missing? And what would it look like if I designed learning experiences with the belief that every single student belongs here and can grow here?

Every choice you make—what you frontload, how you group learners, what options you offer—tells a story about what you believe learners need and who you believe can succeed.

Whenever I share my belief that all students can learn at high levels, one question that always comes up is whether that means all students will perform in exactly the same way. The answer is no. Humans are not identical, and no one is suggesting that we all share the same strengths. There will be a student who can solve the most complex mathematics problems, a student who earns the top score on the SAT, and a student whose voice rises above them all in the school choir. UDL celebrates this richness of human variability, and it affirms that regardless of our unique strengths, every learner deserves access to the same high-quality learning opportunities.

What is often described as an achievement gap is more accurately an opportunity gap. Some students currently have consistent access to rigorous coursework taught through innovative, engaging pedagogy, and others have not had that access yet. We must hold the belief that every student deserves that access and will thrive in an environment that both challenges them and helps them build their agency as learners.

One of my favorite ways to illustrate the importance of access is to imagine that everyone reading this joins a fitness studio. Naturally, there will be variability in our starting points: our cardiovascular fitness, strength, and endurance. Regardless of where we begin, we can all work toward the shared goal of getting stronger and healthier. We might train at the same time, with the same coaches, using the same equipment. But here is the spoiler: We will not all bench-press four hundred pounds. Some of us might (not me), but that is not the point. The point is that we all have the opportunity to grow, and none of us should be excluded because someone assumed from the start that we could not reach a certain milestone.

Every school system will have students who currently perform at the very highest levels, and that is not the issue. The problem is that we can predict who those students will be because they have historically been given the greatest opportunities to learn and the most support. Equity means not lowering expectations but increasing access so that every learner can discover their passions, grow their strengths, address their challenges, and apply those skills to a life, education, and career that are meaningful and fulfilling.

UDL as a Framework for Belief-Driven Planning

If we are going to universally design an environment that gives all students opportunities to learn at high levels, we need to talk about theory. And I know, I know—*theory* sounds like something that belongs in a doctoral program or printed on a mug in the faculty lounge. But stay with me. This isn't about sounding fancy or getting technical. A theory, at its core, is simply a way to explain how things work. It helps us make sense of complexity, organize our thinking, and make more intentional decisions. And the theory behind UDL? It's that all students can learn at high levels when we get the conditions right. But a theory is not enough. We need a theoretical framework to support us.

One of the most widely studied theoretical frameworks in motivation science is self-determination theory.[1] This theory suggests that people are more likely to engage, persist, and thrive when three basic needs are met: autonomy (having a voice and control), competence (believing they can succeed), and relatedness (feeling seen and valued). When those needs are met? Students show up with more confidence, curiosity, and ownership. When they're not? We get disconnection, resistance, or quiet disengagement.

UDL builds directly on this foundation. It's not just a set of strategies. When we choose to approach planning through the lens of UDL, we shift our mindset to one that affirms every student

1 Edward L. Deci and Richard M. Ryan, *Intrinsic Motivation and Self-Determination in Human Behavior* (Plenum Press, 1985).

should have access to autonomy, competence, and connection. Not just some of them. Not just when they behave a certain way or meet some minimum entry criteria. All of them. Every day.

The theory of action behind UDL is simple and powerful: If we define firm goals, identify and remove barriers to those goals, and design flexible pathways for students to engage, learn, and show what they know, then more learners succeed—not just in test scores but in agency, engagement, and belonging. That's also why UDL isn't a checklist. It's not "Did I add a video and a graphic organizer?" It's a mindset shift.

Our beliefs have power. And they don't always work in our favor. When we assume a student should be able to do something a certain way, that assumption can quietly become a barrier. Even in the early years, these beliefs are evident in how we decide when to allow invented spelling, who gets to read aloud, or how we respond to intense emotions during learning moments. When a student disengages or is not successful, it's easy to jump to frustration instead of pausing and asking what we can redesign to improve the situation. We all have those moments. The goal isn't to avoid them. It's to notice them, name them, and see if we can learn from them. Try these questions at your next team meeting, especially when you hear "They're just not getting it":

- What am I assuming this student should be able to do and why?
- Could there be a barrier in the way I've designed the task, environment, or expectations?
- What does this student need more of? Time, clarity, practice, connection, or another way in?
- If I believed this student was fully capable, how might I redesign this moment?

Those are belief-based questions. And they get to the core of UDL. Before we talk strategy, we have to be clear about what we believe.

A *tenet* is a core principle we accept as true and that shapes our learning design. UDL rests on three foundational tenets that often require a shift in beliefs and habits: learner variability is the rule, we should pursue firm goals with flexible means, and building learner agency is essential.

1. **Variability is the rule.** Every class is full of learners with different strengths, needs, languages, interests, and lived experiences. That means we have to stop designing for the so-called average and start planning for a range of learners from the outset. Just as important, performance fluctuates *within* the same learner from moment to moment and day to day. A 2024 study in the *Journal of Cognition* analyzed seven million trials across eleven tasks and found that these within-person changes are real and reliable, distinct from average performance, and not explained by a single mechanism (e.g., attention, fatigue, strategy choice, or task demand).[2] The realities of interpersonal and intrapersonal variability necessitate that we, as designers, plan for flexibility from the start.
2. **Set firm goals with flexible means.** UDL asks us to name clear, firm goals that drive instruction. Those goals must remain at a high level and be visible for every student because access to rigorous, grade-level standards and clarity about them are essential for success. Education researcher John Hattie's *Visible Learning* synthesizes more than 2,100 meta-analyses across over 132,000 studies and roughly 300 million students to pinpoint what most consistently

2 Nicholas Judd et al., "Interindividual Differences in Cognitive Variability Are Ubiquitous and Distinct from Mean Performance in a Battery of Eleven Tasks," *Journal of Cognition* 7, no. 1 (2024): 45, https://doi.org/10.5334/joc.371.

improves achievement.[3] In that model, an effect size of 0.40 is equivalent to about one year of academic growth. Teacher clarity—making learning objectives and success criteria explicit and checking for understanding against them—shows a large effect of about 0.75, which can approach two years of growth when done well. This is where flexibility comes in. To help all students work toward clear goals, we need to design multiple ways to engage, represent essential content, and demonstrate understanding. The aim is not to make learning easier; it is to make learning accessible and effective. Research on student autonomy shows consistent overall positive effects when teachers offer choices within clear expectations,[4] and accessibility studies show that flexible supports (such as multiple representations, graphic organizers, text-to-speech, and captions) improve comprehension and performance for many learners, including students with disabilities.[5] Taken together, the evidence explains why firm goals with flexible means works. Expectations remain explicit and high, instruction remains aligned with the goal, and learners have varied, well-designed pathways to reach it.

3. **Learner agency is essential.** Agency is students' capacity to set goals, reflect, and act to influence their learning and world. This ability is developed in partnership with adults and peers. Evidence shows that when teachers provide autonomy support and well-designed choices, students' intrinsic motivation, persistence, and performance improve

3 John Hattie, *Visible Learning: The Sequel—A Synthesis of Over 2,100 Meta-Analyses Relating to Achievement* (Routledge, 2023).

4 Sakhavat Mammadov and Kayla Schroeder, "A Meta-Analytic Review of the Relationships Between Autonomy Support and Positive Learning Outcomes," *Contemporary Educational Psychology* 75 (2023): 102235, https://doi.org/10.1016/j.cedpsych.2023.102235.

5 Douglas D. Dexter and Charles A. Hughes, "Graphic Organizers and Students with Learning Disabilities: A Meta-Analysis," *Learning Disability Quarterly* 34, no. 1 (2011): 51–72, https://doi.org/10.1177/073194871103400104.

across settings and age groups. When students understand what they're working toward and have some choice in how they get there, they're more motivated, more invested, and more likely to persist.

In practice, applying these tenets means asking hard but helpful questions during planning:

- **Variability:** Am I planning with the full range of learners in mind or just the ones I feel most confident supporting?
- **Clarity and flexibility:** Am I clear on the goal and success criteria, or am I overly focused on the task or the path to reach the goal?
- **Agency:** What options do students have to personalize their learning? How does the design of this lesson give students practice using the skills they will need to be successful in their futures?

We're not going to get this right every time. And that's OK. Shifting beliefs and changing design habits take time. But the more we ask these kinds of questions, about what we believe, what we assume, and how we plan, the more intentional and inclusive our teaching becomes and the more we move beyond simple strategies to strategic planning for all learners.

LEADERSHIP LENS

Just like students, educators thrive when they have flexible pathways to reach firm goals. As leaders, it's easy to fall into one-size-fits-all approaches to professional learning—expecting every teacher to learn the same way, at the same pace, with the same supports. But if we believe in UDL for students, we have to extend that belief to the adults who serve them.

Creating flexibility for teachers might mean offering multiple ways to engage in professional learning: a live workshop, a recorded session, or collaborative planning time with colleagues. It might mean designing coaching cycles that adapt to the needs of different teams. Perhaps it's giving teachers the choice to pilot strategies that align with their goals before scaling schoolwide. When we provide varied supports for educators, we build the same autonomy, competence, and connection that we hope they'll build for students.

As a leader, reflect on the structures you've created for adult learning. Do teachers have options that honor their strengths and needs? Are you creating space for experimentation and feedback? Flexibility isn't about lowering expectations for teachers; it's about creating the conditions where they can thrive, innovate, and sustain the work of inclusion.

I recently read *The Let Them Theory* by Mel Robbins,[6] and while the book is about relationships and boundaries, I couldn't stop thinking about the two sides of the theory as it relates to teaching and learning. In her book, Robbins explains that *let them* is about releasing the need to control other people's actions, choices, or emotions. Instead of stepping in to micromanage or fix, you step back, observe, and allow people to have their own experiences. The idea is that when we *let them*, we give others the space to learn from their choices and take ownership of their path. The second half of her framework, the *let me*, is about shifting your own energy and attention back to what you can control: how you show up, the environment you create, and the boundaries you hold. In the classroom, I see a beautiful parallel: *Let them* choose how they will learn, explore, and demonstrate understanding. And *let me* create the space that welcomes, challenges, and supports all learners in those choices.

6 Mel Robbins, *The Let Them Theory: A Life-Changing Tool That Millions of People Can't Stop Talking About* (Hay House, 2024).

Let them is about honoring learner voice, agency, and autonomy. *Let me* is about my responsibility as the designer to remove predictable barriers, to offer multiple ways to succeed, and to keep the goals high for everyone. Together, those two commitments build the kind of classroom where every learner can thrive in their own way, even if their path looks different from someone else's.

When Beliefs Become Barriers

Often, our strongest instructional routines come from a place of care, clarity, and experience, but when we don't pause to examine them, those routines can quietly become barriers. For example, I used to teach writing with a lot of structure. Every student had to use the same graphic organizer for essays or informative texts. Everyone handwrote their drafts, and five paragraphs were the norm. It felt organized and efficient, and it worked for some students. But looking back, it was all based on a belief that there was one "right" way to write. And here's the irony: As a professional writer, I don't use a graphic organizer or draft my writing by hand, and I can't remember the last time I even thought about paragraph count.

There's nothing wrong with offering structure. Some students thrive with it. Templates and graphic organizers can be powerful scaffolds. The problem isn't the tools we share; it's the requirement that everyone uses the same tools in the same way. The rigid belief that everyone must use the same format sends an unspoken message: There's only one way to think clearly, one way to demonstrate understanding, one way to be a writer. And that message can become a barrier.

Take handwriting. There is solid, peer-reviewed research suggesting that handwriting supports memory and learning. A 2023 study by researchers at the Norwegian University of Science and

Technology,[7] for example, used high-density EEG to show that handwriting activates more areas of the brain than typing. Interesting? Absolutely. Useful? It can be. But here's the part we need to recognize: That study was done in a lab with adults who already had fluent handwriting skills. It didn't include students with fine motor challenges, physical disabilities, or executive functioning differences. In other words, it told us something about handwriting but not about all learners.

Handwriting can support cognitive development and memory, but only if it's accessible and not a barrier. For some students, the act of handwriting creates so much unproductive struggle that it actually interferes with thinking, learning, and demonstrating understanding. That's why UDL matters. It helps us see the difference between teaching a strategy and requiring a single method. It reminds us that we can value a skill without insisting it's the only path forward.

So yes, teach structure. Share a model. But then step back and ask if there's another way students could do this and still achieve the same goal. UDL isn't about shortcuts. It's about embracing variability and designing access points without compromising the goal. It's about offering multiple on-ramps to reach the same destination and reminding ourselves that if a student's best thinking is trapped behind a pencil grip, we need to rethink the design.

When I say things like this, many educators follow up with a legitimate question: But what if the path a student chooses is less rigorous? It's a fair concern. For instance, I can handwrite, but it's not efficient. I can produce more writing when I type. I mean, can you imagine sending letters home in response to every email you receive? You'd never leave your desk. So here's the deeper question we need to ask: What do we really mean by *rigor*?

7 F. R. (Ruud) Van der Weel et al., "Handwriting but Not Typewriting Leads to Widespread Brain Connectivity: A High-Density EEG Study with Implications for the Classroom," *Frontiers in Psychology* 14 (2024): 1219945, https://doi.org/10.3389/fpsyg.2023.1219945.

Is it more rigorous to handwrite a simple response or to type a powerful, structured, well-supported argument? If the highest cognitive demand is the thinking, organizing, and communicating of ideas, then the medium should support, not limit, that process. Now, if you're a K–1 teacher and your goal is for students to form uppercase and lowercase letters, that's different. Handwriting might be the goal. I'm not here to define your outcomes, only to invite you to be clear about what they are.

When I first became an English teacher, all students were assigned hard copies of classic novels, asked to handwrite five-paragraph essays, and expected to write those essays in a single class period, lest they lose points for unfinished or late work. That was simply the way I was taught and the way I was taught to teach. This environment was clearly not the least restrictive one for all learners, so not every student had an opportunity to be in my classroom.

Let's examine how the practices in my classroom conflicted with UDL's core tenets. First, I relied on a single "right" way to write because structure felt supportive and clear, yet in practice, it overlooked learners' variability in strengths, motor skills, and language. Using the same graphic organizer, handwritten drafts, and a fixed paragraph count created consistency, but it pulled focus from the firm goals of writing to uniform procedures; the real outcomes should have been idea development, use of evidence, organization, and clarity. With one prescribed path, students had fewer meaningful choices, which limited agency and impacted their opportunities to practice self-assessment and strategy building. In short, my beliefs and routines produced a single "correct" method for writing that violated all three tenets at once: It denied variability, fixed the method instead of the goal, and removed opportunities for agency. And trust me, it did not result in stellar writing outcomes for all learners, but I didn't know another way to teach writing.

Now, with advances in technology, recognition of flexibility's value, and a focus on student agency, my previous model can be replaced with something far more engaging and inclusive. Take my original novel study. Today, before even reading the novel, I could encourage students to find book trailers online, follow the author on social media, or have a conversation with ChatGPT for five minutes, trying to learn more about why the novel is so acclaimed.

To access the novel, students still have the option of a hard copy, but there are so many more possibilities. They could access an e-book or an audiobook on the public library app or join a reader's theater group with interested classmates. If students don't have library access or if the book isn't available, they can use an iPhone or iPad camera app to convert printed text to digital.

If writing is not the target standard, you could swap out the essay requirement. Students could choose from a written response, a multimedia one like a video or podcast, or a more creative response like visual art with an artist's statement. If writing is the target standard, there can still be options. For example, students could choose to organize their writing using a graphic organizer, a traditional outline, or Post-it notes. To draft, they could write by hand, type their essay, or use voice-to-text. And they could even decide how many paragraphs are most appropriate for the task, purpose, and audience! Providing all these options to all students allows them to create their own strategy, making it far more likely that they will have the conditions they need to be successful.

UDL supports us in shifting conversations from "This student isn't successful in this class" to "They aren't successful yet, which means that these conditions aren't working. What else can I try?" We go from "If students really care, they'll do it this way" to "Because I care so much, I'll make sure they have a way in."

UDL supports us in shifting conversations from "This student isn't successful in this class" to "They aren't successful yet, which means that these conditions aren't working. What else can I try?"

In a middle school speech and language therapy session, there may be an assumption that students always need to practice expressive or pragmatic language through structured conversation. But for some students, engaging with language in creative, low-pressure ways can increase confidence and communication. UDL invites us to provide options that still require intentional use of language but use methods like scripting and recording a dialogue, narrating a comic strip, or acting out a role-play with a peer.

In a high school history class, we might believe that strong learners take detailed notes to prepare for essays like DBQs. But if students struggle to organize information or keep up with the lecture pace, that belief can become a barrier. UDL invites us to provide optional graphic organizers that break the task into parts (such as identifying historical context, analyzing sources, and categorizing evidence) so students can build those skills without being overwhelmed by the format.

In a vocational nursing class, there may be a belief that proficiency is tied to speed. But expecting every student to master complex, high-stakes procedures like taking vital signs at the same pace can undermine learning. UDL helps us shift that belief by emphasizing clear expectations, flexible pacing, and accessible entry points that support all learners in reaching the goal. Students can still be held to performance benchmarks while moving through the steps at their own pace, with options to watch video tutorials, practice on mannequins, or observe a peer demonstration until they're ready to show their skills with clarity and confidence.

Every educator has routines they trust—formats that feel structured, assignments that feel rigorous, and expectations that feel consistent. But UDL invites us to pause and ask, "Who is this working for?" When we design with purpose and flexibility, we don't lower expectations; we create more ways for students to access and meet them. So, as you reflect on your own practice, ask yourself, "What belief is driving this decision? Is it supporting all learners to grow, or is it time to rethink the design?"

Now that you've reflected on the three core tenets of UDL, it's time to put them to the test, literally, with your students. One of the fastest ways to understand whether your design choices are hitting the mark is to ask the people who matter most: your learners.

The Student Voice Test

At the end of your next learning experience, give students a few quick ways to share their feedback. This can be done on paper, digitally, verbally, or with images, depending on what is most accessible for your group. Ask them three questions that align with the three core beliefs:

- "What is one way you learned today that worked really well for you?"
- "If you could change one part of today's lesson, what would it be? Why?"
- "What is one strategy you chose that helped you today?"

Collect the responses and look for patterns. The trends you spot will be a goldmine for planning, helping you keep what's working and rethink what may not be yet. And this strategy works great for adult learners, too. One of my favorite prompts to include in an exit ticket is this sentence frame: "In a follow-up session on this topic, it would be great if . . ." I get my best ideas from educators' responses. If you work with adult learners, try it!

Your Move: Embrace Beliefs

Reflect on your core beliefs about students and learning and how those beliefs align with the UDL framework's core tenets. Choose one or two prompts below and respond in your preferred format: Jot notes, record a voice memo, or talk it out with a colleague.

- When have I underestimated a learner, and what did I learn from that moment?
- What's a belief I used to hold that I've now shifted, and what made the difference?
- When I reflect on the moments I've truly believed in each learner's potential, what helped me hold on to that belief, and how can I build more of those moments into my practice?

Up Next

We've spent this chapter unpacking how beliefs impact action and aligning those beliefs to the core UDL tenets: recognizing variability, designing with firm goals and flexible means, and the importance of building learner agency. We've seen how shifting our mindset shapes our instructional choices and helps us design proactively for all learners. Now that we understand that our beliefs about our students (and ourselves) are the true starting point, it's time to translate those beliefs into actionable design. That's where the UDL principles and resulting UDL Guidelines come in. They offer research-informed lenses to plan for the widest range of learners from the start.

CHAPTER 3

What the Science Really Says

How the Brain Works (and What That Has to Do with Sprinklers)

My husband, Lon, who our friends affectionately call Lawn, is deeply passionate about keeping our grass green (hence the nickname). This is no small task. We have four kids who play lacrosse, and they all think it's completely normal to turn the front yard into a full-on practice field. Goals, cones, a hundred balls everywhere—the works. Still, Lon is committed to keeping it looking as close to turf as possible. He's out there on his tractor multiple times a week, and we have a sprinkler system working hard to keep the grass growing.

Let's talk about that sprinkler system for a minute. As wild as it sounds, it's actually a pretty solid analogy for how the brain works. And by now, you know I love a good analogy. Like a sprinkler system, the brain has different parts that each serve a purpose. But for anything to grow, whether it's grass or learning, those parts need to work together.

First, there's the timer or moisture sensor. That's the part that tells the system when to turn on. No signal? No water. Then come the pipes and valves. These control where the water goes and how much each section of the lawn gets. They manage the flow based on need, making sure the right amount reaches the right zones. Finally, there are the sprinkler heads. This is the part you actually see when the system is running. It's how the water gets delivered and distributed.

Now let's bring that back to learning (see figure 3.1).

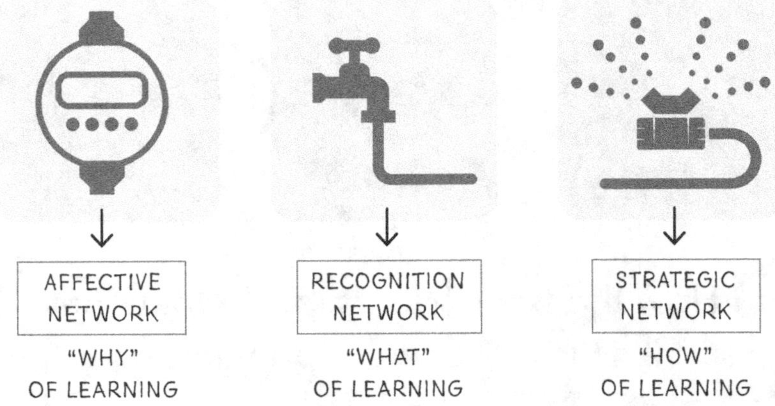

Figure 3.1: Sprinkler System Analogy Illustrating the Three UDL Brain Networks

The timer or sensor is like the affective network. This part of the brain helps us decide what matters, what we care about, and whether something is worth our time. It's the *why* of learning. If there's no purpose, connection, or curiosity, the system doesn't turn on. Research from neuroscience and learning science backs this up. When students don't feel emotionally safe, connected, or interested, the brain doesn't prioritize learning. That's why things like relevance, autonomy, and belonging are essential.

The pipes and valves represent the recognition network. This part of the brain helps us take in information, make sense of it, and connect it to what we already know. It's the *what* of learning. Just like a sprinkler system has to route the flow of water to the right places, the brain has to sort, filter, and organize incoming data, whether it's language, numbers, sounds, or images. If information is only presented in one way, and that way doesn't work for a particular learner, nothing meaningful gets through. That's why UDL pushes us to design content in multiple formats, with support for language, background knowledge, and comprehension.

The sprinkler heads are the strategic network. This is the part we see in action. It's the *how* of learning: how students organize their thoughts, plan next steps, and show what they know. To activate the strategic network, we have to remove unnecessary barriers and, whenever possible, offer more than one way to succeed while also helping students tackle required skills with flexibility and a sense of agency.

Why UDL Aligns with the Science

Back in chapter 1, I shared the "would you rather" technique as a low-lift entry point to more flexible design. It's a small move that empowers educators to offer options to increase flexibility. But here's the thing: Once you understand how the brain's networks work together, even a quick routine like this can become far more intentional. You'll start to think about *which* barriers it removes, how it supports the *why* of learning, and how to extend that same strategy into other parts of your lesson.

That's why understanding the science matters. The more you can see the full system and how engagement, recognition, and action are interconnected, the more strategic you can be about when and how to use flexible options. Just like a sprinkler system needs the timer, pipes, and sprinkler heads working in harmony, learning depends on all three brain networks operating together.

That's why understanding the science matters. The more you can see the full system and how engagement, recognition, and action are interconnected, the more strategic you can be about when and how to use flexible options.

At the core of UDL are three big ideas, or principles, each grounded in how the brain functions. Each one corresponds to a different brain network, and it's important to note that while these networks are distinct in function, they don't work in isolation. For example, when a student writes an informative text, they're not only expressing ideas (strategic network) but also drawing from background knowledge (recognition network) and deciding whether they care enough to put in their best effort and revise (affective network). And just like a sprinkler system, when all three are working together, learning flows.

- **Engagement (the *why* of learning):** This principle aligns with the affective network, the part of the brain that helps us determine whether something is worth our time, attention, effort, and commitment. If students don't feel connected to the learning and aren't willing to engage, they won't. UDL invites us to design learning spaces that acknowledge student variability and provide different ways for students to feel purposeful, curious, and ready and committed to learn.
- **Representation (the *what* of learning):** This principle maps to the recognition network, which helps us take in information, make sense of it, and connect it to what we already know. In learning, if content is only presented in one way, some students may not just miss the idea—they may also struggle with the language, vocabulary, or background knowledge needed to truly understand it. UDL calls us to

provide multiple means of representation, offering content in varied formats and with built-in supports for language and comprehension. That way, every learner has a clearer path to meaning.

- **Action and expression (the *how* of learning):** This principle corresponds with the strategic network, which supports planning, organizing, and expressing understanding. This is where learning becomes visible. Students need different ways to show what they've learned in alignment with the standard, leveraging both flexibility and innovative technologies. UDL encourages us to provide those options, not to make things easier but to make success possible in more than one way.

When we design with all three principles in mind, we support the full learning process: building interest and purpose, making sense of new information, and expressing understanding in meaningful ways. But knowing the principles is just the starting point. The real question is *how* do we put them into action? That's where the UDL Guidelines come in, as they translate the brain science into something you can plan with.

The Guidelines as the Blueprint

The UDL Guidelines, first introduced in 2008, were designed to be dynamic and to evolve in response to new research and educator input. Since the initial version 1.0 in 2008, CAST has released four updates. The newest version was published in July 2024. The material is organized into principles, guidelines, and considerations (which replaced what were previously called checkpoints). As you explore the chart (figure 3.2), notice the emphasis on designing options. No single option will work for all learners. These layers provide a flexible, research-informed way to create inclusive learning environments.

Figure 3.2: UDL Guidelines 3.0

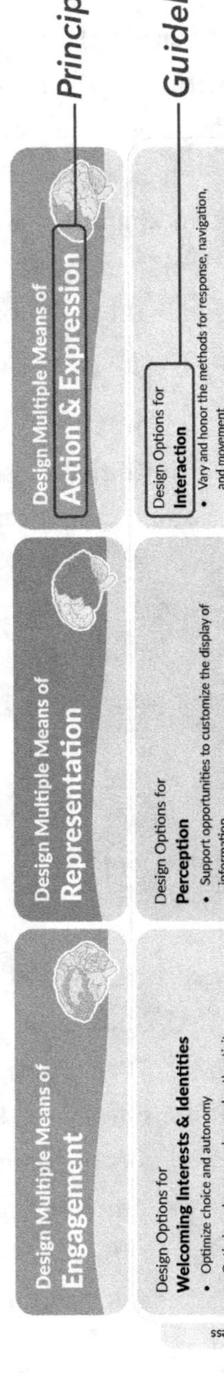

And yes, the UDL Guidelines are backed by extensive research. When we use the UDL framework to interpret that research, it becomes clear that inclusive design isn't just good practice—it's necessary for effective learning. And the most recent version of the UDL Guidelines (3.0) goes even further by incorporating research from inclusive education, disability studies, and asset-based pedagogies.

For example, if we want students to engage, we need them to feel welcome, valued, and interested in learning. How do we do that? That's what the considerations are for, and they are based on current evidence and practical application. In the case of welcoming interests and identities best practices include optimizing choice and autonomy, enhancing relevance and authenticity, nurturing joy and play, and addressing bias and threats that interfere with learning.

When I facilitate workshops, I sometimes provide both a printed copy of the UDL Guidelines and a link to the interactive online version at udlguidelines.cast.org. Then I ask participants to pause and reflect: What is a predictable barrier you see in your setting? Is it that students don't feel interested in your subject matter? Do they struggle with the vocabulary? Do they give up quickly or seem uninterested before you even start? Then we examine the nine guidelines—what I consider predictable barriers—and identify the one that feels most closely aligned with the issue. From there, we explore the considerations. Each one is a research-informed lever that provides ideas you can implement immediately.

From Framework to Action

Some educators look at the UDL Guidelines and see so many barriers that they want to redesign everything all at once. And as much as I love the energy behind a total transformation, sustaining that kind of change can be overwhelming. Instead, let's look at what's possible when educators focus on just one predictable barrier and use the guidelines to plan intentionally. These next examples show how even small shifts, grounded in research, can create more inclusive, engaging, and flexible learning environments for all students.

Imagine an elementary science teacher preparing to launch a lesson on plant growth. In previous years, she noticed some students came in excited to share what they already knew, while others seemed disconnected or hesitant to participate. Rather than trying to overhaul the unit all at once (because, let's face it, the prep period isn't long enough for that!), she focuses on one key element: designing options that welcome diverse interests and identities (Guideline 7). Drawing on these considerations, she invites students to choose how they want to engage with the content. Some explore the types of plants used in their cultural meals, others interview a family member about a plant they've cared for, and some watch a video about plant life in different ecosystems. To nurture joy and play, the teacher sets up a collaborative "plant detective" experience in which students observe and record changes in a seedling over time through photos, sketches, or voice recordings. These options allow students to bring their lived experiences into their learning and learn in ways that feel meaningful and affirming.

Now, let's imagine a middle school guidance counselor preparing a series of small-group sessions to help students manage stress and build emotional resilience. In previous years, she had noticed that some students were fully engaged in discussions, while others remained quiet or avoided sessions altogether. This time, following the UDL Guidelines, she grounds her design in emotional capacity, with a focus on developing awareness of self and others. Rather than using a single set of reflection prompts or assuming every student feels comfortable speaking in a group, she creates multiple ways for students to explore their emotions. Some students use art to depict their stressors, others respond to journal prompts in a shared digital space, and a few prefer one-on-one check-ins to reflect verbally. To make the content more culturally responsive, she integrates examples of different ways people across cultures express and cope with stress, creating space for students to share practices from their own families and traditions. This shift doesn't require more sessions, just a more intentional design that builds safety, honors variability, and helps students develop a deeper awareness of their own needs and emotions.

Now, picture a high school English teacher preparing his students to write literary analysis essays. In the past, some students dove right in while others got stuck, overwhelmed by the structure and unsure how to begin. To better support all students in building their writing stamina, he focuses on developing effective strategies. He begins by offering multiple ways for students to set meaningful goals for their writing: Some choose to focus on organization, others on developing their argument, and a few on building voice or fluency. To support students in organizing their ideas, he shares a range of tools, including graphic organizers, exemplars, and rubrics. He also builds in moments for students to reflect on their process and assess their progress. By designing options for how students develop and monitor their chosen strategies, he helps build agency without sacrificing rigor.

LEADERSHIP LENS

As leaders, we have an incredible opportunity to model UDL in our leadership practices. For example, imagine a high school principal who notices that professional learning sessions tend to feel one-size-fits-all. Some teachers are energized, while others disengage. Rather than defaulting to another lecture-style training, the principal provides educators with multiple options for engaging with the content through varied formats aligned with the guideline for perception.

At the beginning of the session, teachers choose whether they want to read an article, listen to a podcast, or watch a video. Afterward, they each create an individual implementation plan, setting a goal for how they'll apply the strategy in their own context. By offering flexibility and honoring professional autonomy, leaders can model what it means to design with variability in mind. For more ideas about how to implement UDL in professional learning, use the QR code at the beginning of the book to access a tool: Planning Professional Development Using A UDL Lens.

In all these scenarios, learners are more engaged and self-directed. We end up with more collaboration, more options, and more reflection. Instruction becomes more responsive, learning becomes more inclusive, and everyone—educators and students—has more opportunities to succeed. That's the promise of Universal Design for Learning. It's not about doing everything at once. It's about starting somewhere, designing with intention, and trusting that every small shift adds up to meaningful, lasting change.

Your Move: Put the Science to Work

Understanding the science is only the first step. What matters most is how we use that knowledge to reflect on our own design decisions and identify small, powerful shifts we can make in our classrooms and schools.

Take a few minutes to consider one or more of the following questions:

- Where in my current practice am I offering students multiple pathways to success? Where might I be unintentionally creating barriers?
- What's one predictable barrier I see in my setting? Which UDL guideline might help me plan differently next time?

- How can I use this framework not just for lesson planning but for shaping the overall learning environment?

Up Next

We've explored how the brain learns and how the UDL Guidelines translate that science into practical strategies. Now that we've named the problem with one-size-fits-all planning and introduced UDL as a flexible, inclusive alternative to more traditional pedagogy, let's get to work. In chapter 4, we'll explore what it actually looks like to design with intention. Spoiler alert: We're baking a Black Forest cake, not just adding water and eggs to a box mix. You'll see how small, practiced steps can build toward a more flexible, inclusive, universal design.

PART 2

Getting the Conditions Right

CHAPTER 4

Why Planning Needs Practice

From Bake-Offs to Black Forests

I love cooking shows. It's somewhat ironic because no one who knows me would describe me as a chef in any way, shape, or form. My idea of a delicious dinner is a bag of Caesar salad with pulled rotisserie chicken on top. That being said, I absolutely love *Food Network Magazine*, scrolling through online recipes, and watching *The Great British Bake Off*. In each season of the show, twelve incredibly talented amateur bakers compete against each other to win the title of Greatest British Baker. Seriously, if you haven't seen it, these people are wizards when it comes to baking, and they aren't competing for any cash prize. It's straight-up bragging rights, so the real magic is the intrinsic motivation they have to refine their craft.

In season 12, a contestant named Chigs Parmar, a self-taught home baker who had learned from watching YouTube videos (how very UDL!), made it to the finals. One of his creations was a Black Forest imprimé dessert. In the description of the recipe, you are warned, "You'll need patience because it will put your baking skills to the test, but the stunning effects of the finished bake will make every bit of effort worthwhile." I feel like this description works for teaching, too.

The recipe includes thirty-one ingredients, broken into six different cake components: the decorative paste, chocolate joconde, homemade cherry juice, cherry mousse, chocolate bavarois, and decoration. I'm not too proud to admit I had to look up the terms *joconde* and *bavarois* as they relate to baking. After the list of ingredients, there are twenty-seven steps. Yes, twenty-seven. Now, thanks to the internet, all of us have access to this recipe, and if someone gave us a gift card to a grocery store, we could gather all the ingredients and give it our best effort. But here's the thing: Having the recipe doesn't guarantee success for any of us. Why? Well, I can't speak for all of you, but I can speak for myself. Black Forest cake is not a recipe I am familiar with, and the steps in the process are not skills I have practiced. My first attempts would be more appropriate for the show *Nailed It!*

To make something even halfway decent, I would need some significant scaffolds plus my bestie, Kate, who is a talented baker. And I'd need opportunities to try, try, and try again. I have no doubt that eventually I would get something much better than when I started, but I might never perfect the recipe. It doesn't mean that I wouldn't be able to build a solid skill set, but I don't have it yet, and that is OK.

Now let's contrast Chigs's masterpiece with something like a boxed cake mix. It's easy. It's fast. It's predictable. You just add eggs and water. But if you've ever watched *The Great British Bake Off*, you know that real baking isn't about convenience. It's about skill, intention, and knowing how different ingredients work together. UDL invites us to design with more complexity and intention from the start, ensuring more students have what they need to reach their highest potential.

Now, clearly, teaching is inherently more complex than baking. Unlike a recipe that remains consistent, we're working with dynamic humans, each unique and constantly evolving. Just when we feel we've mastered a technique, new ingredients (like emerging technologies or updated standards) and techniques (like new research on cognitive science) emerge, requiring us to continuously adapt and grow. This constant evolution shouldn't feel like a burden. Instead, think of it as an invitation to deepen our craft and expand our impact.

Both judges on the show, Paul Hollywood and Prue Leith, are expert bakers who coach the contestants in each competition, providing praise and guidance as well as action-oriented, constructive feedback to ensure each baker improves every week. Although teaching is not, and should not be, a competition, it's incredibly important to have guidance when pushing your skill set and trying something new. Like the bakers on the show, we're constantly experimenting, tweaking ingredients, adjusting pacing, and learning from what works and what doesn't. But we can't do it alone. Feedback, collaboration, and the willingness to try again are what move us forward.

The Skill Set of Flexibility

We've rejected one-size-fits-all. Now let's explore what it *really* looks like to design differently. Too often, we treat flexibility as something we either have or don't. But like any skill, it can be learned, practiced, and strengthened over time. We build it by trying something new, reflecting on what worked, and gradually integrating those practices into our daily routines.

If this feels messy, that's because it is. And that's OK. Trying something new in your teaching, especially when it's for the benefit of students who've historically been excluded, is not failure; it's growth. It takes courage to teach in a way you weren't taught and to design for needs you may not have personally experienced. That courage is the beginning of inclusive practice. You don't need to be perfect. You just need to be willing to try, reflect, and try again.

> ***If this feels messy, that's because it is. And that's OK. Trying something new in your teaching, especially when it's for the benefit of students who've historically been excluded, is not failure; it's growth.***

I recently read the book *Atomic Habits* by James Clear. I devoured it, learning so much about the power of repetition and habits. I found myself often opening the notes app on my phone to jot down anecdotes, research examples, and statistics that jumped out at me. Here's one that struck me:

> Once a habit has been established, however, it's important to continue to advance in small ways. These little improvements and new challenges keep you engaged. And if you hit the Goldilocks Zone just right, you can achieve a flow state. A flow state is the experience of being "in the zone," and fully immersed in an activity. Scientists have tried to quantify this feeling. They found that to achieve a state of flow, a task must be roughly 4% beyond your current ability.[8]

OK, I feel like it would be pretty challenging to figure out exactly what 4 percent beyond your current ability is, but each of us has our own baseline that we need to build from as we shift to a more universally designed practice. So, I'm translating the 4 percent as baby steps, every day. Let's say you're used to whole-group exit tickets. This week, what if you offer students two ways to reflect at the end of

8 James Clear, *Atomic Habits: An Easy & Proven Way to Build Good Habits & Break Bad Ones* (Avery, 2018), 231–232.

class: a short written response or a quick audio note. That's a 4 percent (ish) shift. Commit to trying this shift every day and measuring its impact at the end of the week. This is doable and a great way to begin offering choice, much like the "would you rather" strategy we explored in chapter 1. These small experiments help you practice and figure out what options resonate with students.

So, back to the recipe/lesson analogy. Imagine I'm presenting in your school or district and I share a universally designed lesson in your subject area with thirty-one materials, scaffolds, and assessment components and twenty-seven steps. Some of these steps will require student reflection, blended learning, and the design of linguistic, conceptual, and sociocultural scaffolds. You may say, "*Love* this. I'm ready to try this," or you may say, "What exactly does it mean to design a conceptual scaffold? I'm not familiar with that language." That same lesson has the potential to inspire and overwhelm. Either way, you will benefit greatly from opportunities to unpack, discuss, try components, and get coaching and feedback on your process. Also, you don't have to be perfect in every part of the lesson all at once.

In the Black Forest imprimé dessert, the first step is to make the decorative paste. If you really want to nail the dessert, practice making the paste every day until you get that right before moving on to the chocolate joconde. When you see a universally designed lesson, it doesn't mean that you need to take that lesson and integrate all of the strategies and flexibility right away. Use it as an opportunity to reflect on how it relates to your own content area, grade level, and role. Then consider what ingredients you have already and which you will need to acquire over time.

Let's unpack a couple of examples of what intentional design can look like in different contexts. Most of these contexts won't align with your role or content area, but you can still reflect on the pedagogy and consider how you can integrate small changes in your own learning environment.

First, let's start with the littlest learners. Imagine a pre-K classroom that is exploring textures. The teacher might set up a sensory bin filled with rice, water beads, and sand, then offer students a choice of tools for scooping and pouring. Some children grab measuring cups, others go for big shovels, and a few dive in with their hands. The teacher can ask students to explain the choices they made to peers by modeling or sharing.

In a middle school PE class, a teacher could introduce a fitness circuit and let students decide whether to start with jumping jacks, bodyweight exercises, or resistance bands. Students could also choose the amount of weight or the strength of the resistance band, adjusting the challenge to match their own strength, stamina, or comfort level. Even though all students work through all three stations, they personalize their fitness journey. At the end of the class, they log their progress on paper or digitally and reflect on how effectively they challenged themselves.

In a high school automotive technology class, the instructor could introduce a vehicle with a mystery performance issue. Students have access to several diagnostic tools, like a digital scanner, a visual inspection checklist, and a test-drive protocol, and they can decide which method to start with, knowing they'll eventually need to cross-check their results. The goal is the same for everyone: to diagnose the issue accurately and justify the process. But the path to get there is up to the learners, allowing them to explore different tools and share their process with each other.

In all the scenarios above, teachers embraced student differences and started by offering multiple ingredients and pathways. Consider how you can embed more flexibility in your lesson design process to find that magic 4 percent so you can continue to grow. This growth, over time, will help you to become the best educator possible for the greatest number of students. Because, as James Clear reminds us in *Atomic Habits*, "The secret to getting results that last is to never stop making improvements. It's remarkable what you can build if you just don't stop."[9]

Shifts in Instruction: Then vs. Now

The reality is that for most of us, this way of teaching wasn't how we were trained. We were taught to follow a plan, deliver content, and keep the pace moving. That's not a critique; it's just the reality of what teacher prep looked like for many of us (me included!). So if designing flexible, inclusive learning still feels unfamiliar or if creating a classroom like the ones in the anecdotes above makes your stomach flip, you're not behind. You're just evolving with the field.

I received my master's in teaching in 2003. I remember taking classes that taught me how to plan lessons, manage the classroom, and communicate with families. I don't remember a single lesson on designing flexible learning experiences. As a high school English teacher, I planned by thinking about the materials I would use—the novels, short stories, and poems I would assign. I would often start the lessons with a do-now activity and then launch into my presentation, which at the time included writing things on the overhead projector. For those of you who missed that era, thank your lucky stars. I did what I could to make my classroom fun, and I would argue it was rigorous, but it wasn't flexible or inclusive, yet.

At that time, technology wasn't readily available, so creating a more innovative experience required me to reserve the computer lab weeks in advance. Now, with 1:1 devices, artificial intelligence becoming an everyday tool, and classrooms more diverse and inclusive than ever, the instructional landscape has fundamentally changed. Our students live in a world of instant information and

9 Clear, *Atomic Habits*, 97.

personalized experiences. The rigid, one-size-fits-all models of my early career simply don't align with this reality, nor do they adequately prepare students for a future that demands adaptability and agency. This isn't just about integrating new tech; it's about rethinking how we design learning to meet the inherent variability that is now the norm, not the exception.

Let's return to our baking analogy. It's like you were trained to be a pastry chef, and then you have to learn Italian cuisine. Of course, you have a strong skill set in cooking, but you need to learn many new recipes and techniques, and that will take commitment and practice. That is where many educators are now.

In some ways, UDL is simple. We have to design instruction so all kids can learn, and to do this, we have to move away from one-size-fits-all instruction, as it doesn't work for everyone. But what does this actually look like? Let's dive into a lesson makeover in high school mathematics. Now, I know most readers are not high school math teachers. The content may differ in your setting, but the principles remain the same: Identify the barriers, stay focused on the learning goal, and provide multiple pathways for students to achieve it. That's the heart of universally designed instruction.

In some ways, UDL is simple. We have to design instruction so all kids can learn, and to do this, we have to move away from one-size-fits-all instruction, as it doesn't work for everyone.

From Recipes to Routines: Planning with Intention

If baking a Black Forest imprimé requires practice, patience, and precision, planning universally designed lessons requires the same. UDL isn't about improvising; it's about designing with intention. The more we practice, reflect, and refine, the more fluent we become in anticipating learner variability and designing for it from the start.

To help us move from theory to action, the UDL Lesson Planning Protocol offers a clear, seven-step process for turning the UDL core tenets and guidelines into daily practice. This process was designed with my team, and we have used it to support tens of thousands of educators to plan differently. Think of it as a recipe for designing a lesson through the UDL lens. It does not replace your professional judgment; it helps you structure it so design is more intentional and proactive. (See chapter 10 for a deeper dive into the protocol.)

The Seven Steps of Intentional Design

1. **Clarify the purpose:** Begin with a clear, grade-level goal that's meaningful to learners. When students understand what they're learning and why it matters, they're more likely to persist through challenges.
2. **Anticipate variability:** Expect differences in background knowledge, language, and motivation. Identify likely barriers (you can use the UDL Guidelines to help predict barriers) and plan to minimize those barriers by integrating the UDL considerations.
3. **Build a welcoming start:** As you think about lesson design, identify how you will establish belonging and relevance from the first minutes. Create entry points that connect to students' experiences and invite them to engage.

4. **Design flexible assessments:** Great design is backward design, so before you start thinking about how students will learn, consider how they will ultimately share what they know. At this stage, design multiple ways to show what learners know and align these closely with the grade-level learning objectives articulated in step 1.
5. **Design flexible learning experiences:** As you continue to think about student variability, plan for active learning through multiple pathways. Consider multiple means of representation, opportunities to collaborate, and the value of embedded small-group instruction using formative assessment data. That way, every student can reach the learning objective.
6. **Create space for student ownership:** As you think about the lesson, be sure to embed reflection, feedback, and goal-setting throughout so learners monitor their own growth and begin to co-design their learning experiences.
7. **Plan an intentional close:** Always consider how you will end the lesson purposefully. Reinforce mastery, celebrate effort, and create closure so students leave with clarity and confidence about their progress.

These steps aren't about perfection—because goodness knows nothing is about perfection. They're about iteration. Each cycle of planning and reflection helps us move closer to designing instruction that's as intentional as it is inclusive. Just as I'm sure Chigs practiced layer by layer to perfect his Black Forest imprimé, we strengthen our instructional craft by practicing these design habits, one layer at a time.

Lesson Makeover: From One-Size to Universally Designed

Let's make this concrete by walking through a universally designed lesson makeover anchored in a high school algebra standard: Graph linear and quadratic functions and show intercepts, maxima, and minima.

This standard requires students to analyze quadratic functions by identifying and interpreting key features of their graphs, a skill that requires both procedural fluency and conceptual understanding. It's a rich, complex goal, but it's one that can become inaccessible if taught through a one-size-fits-all approach.

In a traditional version of this lesson, the ingredients might include whiteboards and markers, printed worksheets, and calculators. The flow of the lesson may go something like this: The teacher kicks things off by welcoming students and modeling key concepts related to quadratic functions while learners take notes. After the mini-lesson, students pair up to work on a problem using whiteboards to show their thinking. To wrap things up, students work independently on a printed worksheet while the teacher circulates to offer support and feedback.

It is an absolutely solid lesson, but because it's one-size-fits-all, it may not be accessible to all students. For example, imagine the classroom has students with significant intellectual support needs, L1 language learners who don't read or speak English yet, or students who haven't yet met prerequisite math standards. In this scenario, linguistic and conceptual barriers exist that would need to be addressed through the design process so all students can learn. So this is what my team and I set out to do.

To create UDL math guidelines, I collaborated with two math education experts: Karen Gartland is a career math educator and retired faculty member at Lesley University, and she is the author of five math education books. Dr. Nathan Lang-Raad is the author of ten books, including the newly released *Mathematics Teaching Reimagined: Seven Competencies to Foster Robust Student Learning and Engagement*. (Lang-Raad's book is about design considerations that math teachers can leverage to build more accessible and flexible classrooms). We will examine some of these math guidelines and how they can help create more access and entry points, increased engagement, and greater flexibility for students in the algebra lesson. You can access the full UDL Math Guidelines using the QR code at the beginning of the book.

For this particular lesson makeover, I collaborated with the brilliant Elizabeth Kielty, a high school math specialist from the All Learners Network whose work focuses on making rigorous mathematics accessible to every student. Together, we designed this example to resonate with high school math teachers and to show how a traditional, one-size-fits-all lesson can be transformed into one that is universally designed.

Step 1: Clarify the purpose

The first step is to clarify the instructional goal, but before students dive into vocabulary like *vertex* or *intercepts*, the teacher anchors the learning in a shared context that makes the math meaningful. For example, the teacher might show an image of a player taking a shot at a varsity basketball game and invite students to make observations and generate mathematical questions such as "What shape do you notice is created by the path of the basketball?" and "How could we predict or design that path?" This context serves as a touchstone throughout the lesson, providing a real-world frame of reference as students develop a conceptual understanding of quadratics.

Once curiosity is sparked, the teacher and students co-construct meaning around the learning goals by unpacking the standard (graph linear and quadratic functions and show intercepts, maxima, and minima). Together, they translate and discuss the learning target in clear, student-friendly objectives such as these:

- I can identify the vertex, intercepts, and axis of symmetry of a quadratic function.
- I can explain how the equation of a function connects to its graph.

At this stage, the teacher facilitates a brief discussion about the objectives and why they matter. The focus is on building a shared understanding of the lesson's purpose. Later, once students have explored the concept through context and practice, the teacher and class can revisit the criteria together to clarify what meeting the goal looks like in action.

Step 2: Anticipate variability

The teacher anticipates diverse levels of readiness, language proficiency, and confidence. Variability shows up in countless ways—not just in skill levels but in students' lived experiences, interests, and methods of representing ideas. To proactively design for this predictable variability, the teacher can follow this guidance:

- Include previously introduced representations through short curiosity-building routines like "Which one doesn't belong?" or "Same or different?" or "Find the connection between these two graphs." These small exposures help students notice features and patterns of quadratics before formal instruction begins.
- Predict likely misconceptions, such as confusing intercepts with vertices.
- Use the Frayer Model and anchor charts to explicitly teach mathematical vocabulary.
- Prepare visual scaffolds such as color-coded graphs, manipulatives (e.g., algebra tiles), and interactive digital tools (e.g.,

Desmos) to guide students through the concrete-representational-abstract progression.

By anticipating both gaps and entry points, the teacher positions all students to connect with the math, building familiarity, confidence, and curiosity before abstraction becomes a barrier.

Step 3: Build a welcoming start

A universally designed lesson doesn't start with formulas. It starts with curiosity and connection. The teacher plans the launch with intention by considering these questions:

- What do I want students to notice or wonder about?
- What do I hope they'll talk about?
- How will this discussion position them to meet the learning goal?

As shared above, in this lesson, the teacher shows images of a basketball shot and poses focused questions. To be clear, the launch isn't just a warm-up or do-now activity. It's a purposeful opportunity to reason mathematically, and through the UDL lens, students can share their reasoning in multiple ways. For example, they may talk with a partner, sketch on whiteboards, or jot notes. Because the launch is anchored in a shared context, all learners can access it. Launches like these, that use real-world examples, remove the fear of calculation and create a common entry point for mathematical discourse, particularly for students still developing language or background knowledge.

Step 4: Design flexible assessments

Using backward design, the teacher offers flexible options for demonstrating understanding during the independent task phase. Flexibility is embedded in both the product and how students explain their reasoning. For example, students might be instructed to do any of the following:

- Construct a hands-on model (such as a string parabola, trebuchet, or slingshot) to illustrate how quadratic functions model projectile motion or real-world arcs.
- Write a reflection comparing different methods for solving a quadratic equation, analyzing which approach makes the most sense in various contexts.
- Present a short collaborative "math talk" explaining how they identified a vertex or intercept in a real-world problem.
- Create a visual slide or Desmos presentation that models a quadratic function in a context they design, like predicting the maximum height of a projectile or comparing parabolic arches.
- Record an audio or video reflection explaining their thinking and connections between an equation, a graph, and a real-world context.

By choosing their representation and communication mode, students build both conceptual understanding and agency. This approach shifts assessment from proving mastery to showing reasoning, allowing multiple entry points for diverse learners.

Step 5: Design flexible learning experiences

Now comes the heart of instruction. The teacher uses active, multimodal learning experiences to support access and engagement:

- **Flexible materials:** The teacher provides both hard and digital copies of all math tasks, allowing students to use assistive technologies such as read-aloud features and translation tools to enhance comprehension.
- **Math discourse:** The teacher embeds opportunities for mathematical discourse by modeling productive talk moves

before transitioning to collaborative work. To support this, the teacher provides sentence frames, question prompts, and protocols for students to discuss mathematical reasoning and justify their thinking as they collaborate. This provides students with opportunities to discuss their problem-solving, which aligns with the Standards for Mathematical Practice.

- **Small-group instruction:** In secondary math, small-group instruction isn't always part of the typical classroom routine, but it can be one of the most powerful ways to personalize support and extend learning. When teachers design lessons with formative checkpoints and flexible structures, pulling small groups becomes a natural part of differentiation. During collaborative or independent work time, the teacher uses formative data to meet briefly with students who share a similar need or goal. For example, one group might revisit how to connect a quadratic equation to its graph, while another explores how changes in coefficients affect the shape of the parabola. These moments offer targeted feedback, clarify misconceptions, and deepen understanding through just-in-time support. Importantly, small-group instruction also communicates a powerful mindset shift: Every student in the room deserves access to targeted instruction. In this universally designed classroom, flexible grouping and regrouping give all learners opportunities for enrichment, scaffolding, and connection.

Step 6: Create space for student ownership

Throughout the lesson, students track their progress and reflect using prompts like these:

- What strategy helped you find the vertex most efficiently?
- What errors did you notice, and how did you fix them?

- How does your graph show your understanding of the function?

Rather than relying on traditional note-taking, students engage in note-making, which empowers them to actively organize and personalize what they've learned. The teacher provides structures such as graphic organizers and reflection templates for students to record insights, examples, and strategies in their own words. For example, students may be given these sentence frames:

- Something important from today's task that I need to remember is . . .
- I prefer to use ____ to show my solution because . . .

Students are also encouraged to respond to the prompts in multiple ways, including graphs, tables, equations, verbal explanations, and visual models. This flexibility communicates that there isn't one "right" way to think about or learn math. (There are many!) When teachers invite and validate different pathways, students can develop both mathematical confidence and a sense of identity as problem solvers. By designing space for reflection, choice, and multiple representations, the teacher shifts the classroom from "think like me" to "show me your thinking."

Step 7: Assess, reflect, and close with intention

As the lesson concludes, students return to the anchor context introduced at the start. By revisiting that familiar scenario (i.e., the varsity basketball shot), they can apply what they've learned in more sophisticated ways. For example, students return to the basketball clip and analyze it using their new understanding:

- Where is the vertex in this shot, and what does it represent?
- How would changing the launch angle or speed affect the trajectory of the parabola?

- Can we model this motion with an equation?

In returning to the anchor context, the teacher also revisits the co-created success criteria established at the beginning of the lesson, criteria that now have tangible meaning. Together, the class reflects on how their new insights connect to those criteria:

- How do we identify the vertex, intercepts, and axis of symmetry of a quadratic function?
- How do we explain how the equation of a function connects to its graph?

This return to both the context and the criteria helps students connect procedural fluency and conceptual understanding to a meaningful, memorable story.

Students then extend this understanding through a performance task that allows them to demonstrate mastery in a meaningful and authentic way. For example, they might design and analyze their own quadratic model, like modeling the path of a rocket, the shape of a roller coaster, or the curve of an architectural arch, and use any combination of tools (graphing software, manipulatives, digital media, or paper-based analysis) to show their reasoning and process.

At this point, the teacher intentionally bridges the connection between this rich, authentic work and the standardized assessments students will eventually encounter. Together, the class examines how both types of assessments measure similar skills, such as analyzing graphs, interpreting relationships, and reasoning quantitatively, but at different levels of depth. Students are invited to compare the two, reflecting on questions like these:

- What's the same about the thinking required for this project and for a standardized test problem on quadratics?

- How might a deeper understanding of the concept help me tackle multiple-choice or short-answer questions more effectively?

By exposing students to multiple assessment types, we help them understand the *why* behind the math, which equips them to approach both authentic and standardized assessments with confidence and flexibility.

Finally, students reflect on three levels of learning:

- **About the standard:** What did I learn about graphing and analyzing quadratic functions?
- **About myself as a learner:** What helped me learn best, and what will I try next time?
- **About preparation:** Which study or practice strategies supported my success, and how will I adjust them moving forward?

This intentional close provides both cognitive and emotional closure, grounding abstract mathematics in a memorable story and affirming growth. It shows that deep understanding ultimately drives success on every kind of assessment.

Although these shifts may not seem earth-shattering, they will make a significant difference for all learners. For example, let's imagine my amazing daughter, Aylin, who has an IEP, were enrolled in the classroom with the original lesson design. In that scenario, the teacher would have to design numerous accommodations to create a more inclusive and flexible lesson. It would feel like a lot of work for a single student. In her IEP, Aylin has accommodations that are quite common for students with support needs:

- Clear expectations and/or models or exemplars
- A digital version, as requested
- Read-aloud word problems when requested

- Opportunities to discuss/verbally plan writing

Another common accommodation is "provide a copy of teacher notes" or "fill-in-the-blank notes." While well-intentioned, these practices can unintentionally remove the very thinking we want students to engage in. Instead of copying or filling in missing words, students should have access to structures, models, and discourse that support them in creating their own notes. When students actively construct meaning by summarizing steps in their own words or sketching diagrams, they deepen their understanding and build independence.

With universally designed routines such as flexible note-taking, collaborative discourse, and multiple ways to show thinking, teachers don't have to create separate pathways for students like Aylin. What's necessary for her becomes an option for everyone. Imagine the multilingual learner who thrives with digital translation tools that they can use to review tasks in their native language before accessing them in English. Think of the student who processes information more effectively through math discourse. That's the real power of UDL: It transforms accommodation into design, compliance into cognition, and "extra work" into shared access.

Now, as I said before, I know not everyone is a high school algebra teacher. But the point of this example isn't about quadratic functions. It's about design. Every subject, every grade level, and every role in a school involves opportunities to remove barriers and create more flexible paths for students to meet high expectations. So here's your moment to reflect:

- What's a current lesson, task, or process in your world that might still be operating on a one-size-fits-all model?
- Where do students struggle, disengage, or need extra support just to access the experience?

- How might a few proactive shifts using the UDL Lesson Planning Protocol open up that experience for more learners?

The goal isn't to overhaul everything overnight. It's to start with one lesson, one task, or one routine and ask, "How can I make this just a little more flexible so more students can succeed?"

LEADERSHIP LENS

Leaders send powerful messages through the way they design and facilitate professional learning. If PD is lecture heavy, offers little choice, limits collaboration, or leaves no time for application, the implicit message is that this is what "teaching" looks like. Educators will often mirror the structures they experience.

Before your next PD session or faculty meeting, pause and ask yourself, "If tomorrow a teacher taught a class exactly the way I facilitated today's session, would that be what I want for our learners?"

If the answer is yes—fantastic. If it's not, start your 4 percent improvement journey by implementing one of the ideas that follow, all adapted from an Edutopia article called "Designing a Better Staff Meeting"[10] that I co-wrote with Mike Woodlock, my amazing colleague and the co-author of *UDL Playbook for School and District Leaders*:

- **Prioritize social and emotional well-being.** Recognize that educators bring their whole selves to meetings, and those experiences shape how they connect and engage. Start with an optional check-in that can be done in multiple ways, such as a quick verbal share in small groups, jotting a response on a sticky note, or adding a thought to a visual board. Incorporate elements that make the space feel welcoming and energizing, such as music, humor, images,

10 Katie Novak and Mike Woodlock, "Designing a Better Staff Meeting," Edutopia, September 29, 2021, https://www.edutopia.org/article/designing-better-staff-meeting/.

or light refreshments. Build in moments to listen deeply, acknowledge contributions, and celebrate wins so the meeting supports both professional growth and a strong sense of community.

- **Provide multiple opportunities for staff engagement.** Build in time for colleagues to collaborate, reflect, and move around. Offer choices such as small-group discussion, written reflection, or walk-and-talk conversations. Add short breaks every few slides or agenda items so participants can stretch, grab a snack, or connect with peers while discussing a prompt related to the meeting's goals.
- **Showcase best practices.** Dedicate a few minutes in each meeting for colleagues to share strategies, lesson designs, assessment ideas, or student work. Encourage presenters to share in ways that highlight their strengths, such as live demonstrations, visuals, short videos, or hands-on examples, so peers can access and apply the ideas in different ways. Peer-to-peer sharing builds collective expertise, sparks innovation, and affirms the talents within your community.

When we as leaders design professional learning with the same flexibility, clarity, and accessibility we expect in classrooms, we normalize UDL as a system-wide approach rather than an isolated teaching technique.

Your Move: One Ingredient at a Time

Think of a lesson you recently taught, a meeting you facilitated, or an event coming up on your calendar. Without overhauling the whole thing, choose one or more ingredients you could adjust or add to make it more flexible for your learners. Consider questions like these:

- Would a quick video recap help some learners review?
- Could you offer two ways to demonstrate understanding?
- Could you start with an optional conversation before jumping into independent work?

Pick one change. Try it. See what happens. You don't have to perfect the whole cake. Just start with the decorative paste.

Up Next

In the next chapter, we'll dive more deeply into one of the most powerful ideas at the heart of Universal Design for Learning: firm goals and flexible means. You'll see how setting clear, non-negotiable goals while allowing flexibility in how students reach them transforms teaching and learning. This chapter will help you distinguish between what students need to learn and how they learn and show that learning. That way, you can design lessons that are rigorous, inclusive, and adaptable to every learner's strengths, needs, and interests using the UDL Guidelines and the UDL planning process introduced in this chapter.

CHAPTER 5

Firm Goals and Flexible Means

Magnet Girl and the Side Table

Let me tell you a story about my sister, a lake in Maine, and why I'd draft my brilliant, neurodivergent daughter, Aylin, first if the zombie apocalypse ever hit.

We were enjoying a weekend lakeside in Maine, paddleboarding near the dock. My sister lost her balance and flailed just enough to knock a small metal side table straight into the water. Splash. Gone. No big deal, except that we were renting an Airbnb and would have to either retrieve the table or buy another one. Naturally, my sister and I launched into problem-solving mode. Cue us testing our breath-holding skills and debating visibility and depth to decide who would dive in to retrieve it.

Then along strolls Aylin. She takes one look at our drama and says, "Why don't you just use a fishing magnet?" And sure enough, she comes back with a long rope and a twenty-five-pound magnet she'd packed in case of an emergency (this is what I mean about zombie readiness). A few minutes later? The table's back.

We were so caught up in how we thought the problem had to be solved that we didn't stop to consider all the options. We had a clear goal: Get the table back. But we were locked into one idea of how to do it. Aylin? She knew it was about the outcome, not the method. That, my friends, is what firm goals and flexibility are all about.

Firm Goals: What Stays the Same

Too often, educators are told to "differentiate," "personalize," or "offer choice," but without a clear anchor, that can feel chaotic and unrealistic. Here's where UDL gives us a structure: When you define your learning goals clearly, you can allow for flexibility in how students get there. That's what makes the difference between inclusive design and an educational free-for-all. And it's why the first step of the UDL planning process in the previous chapter is focused on clarifying the purpose of instruction.

UDL has a reputation—which is totally unfair—for being a little loosey-goosey. People hear "flexibility" and assume anything goes. But UDL is incredibly disciplined when it comes to goals and teacher and student clarity. The goals are the non-negotiables. They can be grounded in various sources, such as grade-level state standards, IB or AP requirements, or objectives aligned with transferable skills or outcomes articulated in a Portrait of a Learner. Whatever the source, your goal should be clear and specific enough to define the destination, not the route to get there.

UDL has a reputation—which is totally unfair—for being a little loosey-goosey. People hear "flexibility" and assume anything goes. But UDL is incredibly disciplined when it comes to goals and teacher and student clarity.

Learning Objectives: A Foundation for Engagement

One of the most powerful and practical ways to design for engagement is to ensure that firm, grade-level-aligned learning objectives are clearly visible, referenced throughout instruction, and meaningfully connected to the activities, materials, and assessments in a lesson. This may seem simple, but it's one of the clearest ways to establish purpose and create a foundation for autonomy, competence, and agency. To help educators see what this looks like in practice, my amazing colleagues and I at Novak Education created the UDL Look-Fors tool. This set of eight observable focus areas can be used for reflection, feedback, and observation. You can access the complete UDL Focus Areas observation tool using the QR code at the beginning of the book.

The first focus area in the tool is exactly this: clear learning objectives. Here's what that might look like in practice.

Emerging (1)	Proficient (2)	Shifting to Student-Led (3)
Learning objectives are visible but may not yet fully align with grade-level standards. Connections to instruction, activities, and success criteria are limited or unclear.	Learning objectives are visible, clearly aligned to grade-level standards, consistently referenced throughout instruction, and explicitly connected to activities, materials, assessments, and success criteria.	Teachers and students engage and co-create the learning goal by actively discussing it, defining and annotating any unknown vocabulary to translate it to student-friendly language, and discussing the *why* of learning. Students set authentic, personal goals tied to grade-level objectives, choose their own learning pathways, and use clear success criteria to self-assess and track their progress toward mastery.

Clear goals anchor a lesson, helping students connect what they're doing right now to the bigger picture of their growth. They also give learners a target they can aim for, monitor, and celebrate, whether they're working independently or collaborating with peers. Without that clarity, students may work hard but feel like there's no destination. A clear indicator that you're heading into this territory is a question like "Why are we doing this?" When we communicate clear learning goals, students know where they're headed and can make intentional choices about how to get there.

One way to check if students have that clarity is to ask them directly. Their answers can give you quick insight into whether they understand the purpose of the lesson and see themselves as active participants in reaching the goal. Here are some example questions:

- What are you learning today?
- How will you know you've mastered it?
- What does success look like for you in this lesson?
- Do you have a personal goal for this lesson? Why did you create it? What do you need to do to achieve it?

Questions like these not only reveal whether students grasp the goal, but they also help learners develop the habit of reflecting on their own learning. Which brings us to an important distinction: When we talk about a goal, what exactly do we mean? There are two types of goals: content goals and method goals.

Content Goals

Content goals show a student has attained knowledge, and pretty much all content goals are synonymous with "Students need to understand this." Certainly, there are different levels of knowledge, but the key to the content standard is that it doesn't explicitly specify how students should share their understanding.

Many educators are familiar with Webb's Depth of Knowledge (DoK),[11] which outlines four escalating levels of cognitive demand (see figure 5.1). Level 1, Recall, asks learners to remember or locate information. Recall verbs include words like *define* and *identify*. Level 2, Skills and Concepts, requires routine application of knowledge such as compare, organize, or infer. Level 3, Strategic Thinking, pushes students to explain and critique. Level 4, Extended Thinking, involves sustained inquiry and synthesis: Students design, synthesize, and prove original products.

11 Norman L. Webb, et al., *Web Alignment Tool*, Wisconsin Center for Education Research, University of Wisconsin–Madison, July 24, 2005.

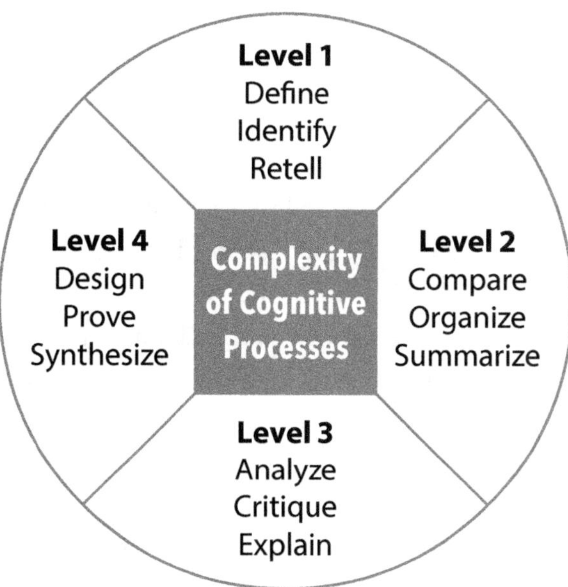

Norman L. Webb, et al. Web Alignment Tool. Madison: Wisconsin Center for Education Research, University of Wisconsin-Madison, July 24, 2005.

Figure 5.1: Depth of Knowledge Levels with Sample Academic Verbs

What you may notice about all the verbs above is that none of them indicate *how* students will define, organize, analyze, or evaluate. Every subject area has these content standards, and they leave lots of room for flexible pathways. This distinction between what students learn (the goal) and how they learn (the means) is a cornerstone of UDL. It empowers us to maintain high expectations for mastery while moving beyond instructional methods that inadvertently exclude learners. As educators, we sometimes decide whether learners explain in writing or analyze in a classroom presentation, even though the firm goals don't necessarily require it. For example, take the content standards below. Review and reflect on all the possible ways students could share their learning.

- **ELA:** Analyze examples of leadership and leaders from history, everyday life, and literature or informational texts (including read-alouds) and describe the qualities of a good leader.

- **Math:** Understand that a two-dimensional figure is congruent to another if one can be obtained from the other by rotations, reflections, and translations; given two congruent figures, describe a sequence showing their congruence.
- **Science:** Apply scientific ideas to construct an explanation for the anatomical similarities and differences among modern organisms and between modern and fossil organisms to infer evolutionary relationships.
- **History:** Identify and explain historical and contemporary efforts to narrow discrepancies between foundational ideas and values of American democracy and realities of American political and civic life.
- **PE:** Evaluate personal fitness measures in relation to patterns of physical activity.
- **Music:** Interpret intent and meaning in a musical work, using specific vocabulary to identify and discuss its details.

When we separate the *what* from the *how*, we protect the integrity of the standard while opening the door to more inclusive and engaging learning. Content goals define the destination—what students need to know and understand—without locking them into a single route for getting there or showing what they know.

One of my favorite techniques when I design a PD session or teach a graduate course on a content standard is to offer three ways to engage with the same content: something to read, something to listen to, and something to watch. I actually started my podcast, *The Education Table*, so I could provide an option for educators to listen to the concepts under study. Each episode is less than ten minutes, which makes it a perfect supplement to reading a short article or blog.

When I give people ten minutes, I tell them they can read a printed article, access it digitally, or take their earbuds and go for a walk or a coffee at the café next door while they listen. They can also watch short videos on the topic. Then we come back together to share what we learned.

I'll never forget a teacher once asking, "Wait—we are allowed to leave?" When highly trained professionals feel trapped in a room for hours, that says a lot about the current state of professional learning. Building in authentic choice when working toward content standards is not about letting people off the hook. It's about trusting learners to choose the mode that best supports their learning.

And just to be clear, you don't need to start a podcast to create options for learners. You can share a digital text with built-in read-aloud tools, use something like NotebookLM to transform a passage into a lively conversation, or even invite upper-grade or older students to introduce themselves and record their readings of the text. There are so many ways to make learning more accessible and engaging for everyone without adding hours to your prep time.

Method Goals

Now that we've covered content goals, let's turn to method goals. These demonstrate that a student has learned how to do something and attained a skill. The goals are action-oriented and often aligned with specific performance expectations, such as writing an argument, solving a multi-step equation, graphing a linear function, conducting a science investigation, or performing a piece of music with accurate tempo and dynamics.

These goals may seem a little less flexible by nature because there's a clear *how* built into them. If the goal is to write an argument, then yes, students need to produce writing. But that doesn't mean they all have to write the same way or use the same tools. Writing can happen with pencil and paper, keyboard and screen, or even talk-to-text platforms that let students generate ideas orally and then revise the transcript. In kindergarten and first grade, when the method goal is to accurately form uppercase and lowercase letters, students might trace in shaving cream, rainbow write with crayons, build letters with playdough, or use finger tracing before they ever pick up a pencil. They're still practicing the same skill but with flexible means.

In a world language class, method goals might include speaking, writing, or interpreting in the target language. If the goal is to retell a story aloud using past-tense verbs, students might choose to record a podcast, act out a skit with a partner, or narrate a storyboard they create on paper or digitally. If the goal is to write a descriptive paragraph in the target language, students could decide whether to type, handwrite, or use voice-to-text, and they might structure it as a traditional paragraph, a poem, or a smash doodle combining visuals and text. For reading goals, students could choose how they access the same high-quality text: independently, with a peer, or with the teacher in a small group. The goal remains firm, whether it's to speak, write, read, or listen in the target language. The means flex to meet learners where they are and help them grow.

In a music class, if the method goal is to play a simple melody on the recorder, and the only instrument that students have access to is the recorder, then yes, all students will need to produce sound with accurate pitch and rhythm. That's the skill we're aiming for. But how they get there can be flexible. Some students might read traditional sheet music, while others rely on color-coded note charts or letter names written on the instrument. One student might benefit from working with a teacher one-on-one, while another prefers looping video tutorials or playing along with a slowed-down track. The goal stays the same: Play the piece. But the journey there can look different.

If you're a service provider, this same truth applies to working with students one-on-one. For example, if the goal is to hold a pencil with control in an OT session, students might explore different grips, choose between vertical or slant boards, or opt for hand-strengthening activities like TheraPutty or rainbow writing. If a student is working toward clear articulation in a speech and language session, they might be given the choice to practice using a mirror or speech app, or they might read silly sentences into a recording tool for playback. If the goal is to work with a counselor to regulate emotions, the student can help co-create a tool kit of strategies such as breathing techniques, drawing, or journaling, then choose which ones to use in the moment. The possibilities are endless!

AI as a Partner, UDL as the Guide

To determine the right level of flexibility in a UDL-aligned lesson, we first need to know whether the outcome we're aiming for is a content goal, a method goal, or a blend of both. While blends aren't especially common, they do exist. Some of the Next Generation Science Standards, for example, combine content and methods: "Develop a model of waves to describe patterns in terms of amplitude and wavelength and that waves can cause objects to move." Here, the goal specifies non-negotiable content and the requirement to develop a model. There can still be flexibility in how students learn about amplitude and wavelength, and in whether their model is physical or digital, but the firm goal defines both the content and the method.

It's tempting to blend standards that aren't intertwined, but that may not give all students opportunities to succeed. When we can identify the true nature of a standard, we can design options that are construct-relevant—aligned to the essence of the goal—rather than layering on activities that may look engaging but don't serve the standard. When we know exactly what must be learned, we can be much more intentional about how students get there and how they show what they know.

Of course, knowing the difference in theory and untangling it in practice are two different things. Some standards are straightforward; others can feel like a knot you can't quite loosen. This is where tools—yes, even robots—can help. Generative AI can be a thought partner to help unpack a standard, clarify the non-negotiables, and brainstorm flexible pathways for learning and expression. The goal isn't to hand over your professional judgment but to use the technology to expand your thinking, spark ideas you might not have considered, and make more space for reflection, experimentation, and innovation. But remember, you always have the last word.

This is especially important in light of a 2025 study from MIT researchers that found overreliance on AI can actually change how our brains work.[12] In the study, researchers used electroencephalograms (EEGs) to monitor participants' brain activity as they completed essay-writing tasks both with and without AI assistance. The EEGs revealed significant differences in brain connectivity patterns between the two conditions. When students relied heavily on AI, there was a noticeable decrease in synchronization between brain regions associated with higher-order reasoning, working memory, and sustained attention. In other words, AI wasn't just doing the work; it was eroding the very mental processes we need for critical thinking (yes, they actually used the word *erode* in the study). Now that is some sci-fi madness if I've ever heard it.

For educators and our students, this is a cautionary tale, not a call to ban every AI tool and retreat to a bunker. AI can be an incredible tool for generating ideas or providing quick feedback, and we should absolutely use it to be more efficient in our thinking process, but we should not substitute it for our own thinking. Knowing that you will need to lean into a conversation to get it just right for your

12 Andrew Chow, "Is Using ChatGPT to Write Your Essay Bad for Your Brain? New MIT Study Explained," *TIME*, June 27, 2025, https://time.com/7298299/chatgpt-bad-for-brain-study/.

learners, here is a simple structure you can use when prompting an AI tool to help you design with more flexibility:

- "What must students know or be able to do to meet this grade-level standard?" (Be sure to copy/paste the entirety of the standard for the most accurate results.)
- "What are three flexible means I could offer students to help them learn or show what they know as they work toward this standard?"

Let's walk through what that might look like in action by unpacking a standard for elementary math: "Given a two-digit number, mentally find 10 more or 10 less than the number, without having to count, and explain the reasoning used."

Prompt	ChatGPT response
What must students know or be able to do to meet this grade-level standard?	• Understand place value, particularly that the tens place changes when adding or subtracting ten, while the ones place stays the same. • Mentally calculate 10 more or 10 less than a given two-digit number without counting one by one. • Explain their reasoning using place value understanding.
What are three flexible means I could offer students to help them learn or show what they know?	1. Math Journal Entry: Write the original number, then record 10 more and 10 less. Use a simple drawing or number line to show how the tens digit changes and explain your thinking in one or two sentences. 2. Audio or Video Recording: Use a tablet or recording device to say your number out loud, then share what 10 more and 10 less would be. Explain your reasoning using place-value language. 3. Interactive Model or Manipulative Demonstration: Use base-ten blocks, Unifix cubes, or a digital tool, such as a place-value chart on a whiteboard app, to demonstrate your thinking. Take a photo or screenshot of your model and write or say a short explanation.

How to Think Critically About This AI Response

Before simply accepting this AI-generated list, it's important to interrogate it: Does it match the exact intent and rigor of the grade-level standard? Do the tasks build toward deep, transferable understanding, or could students complete them without real reasoning? And finally, what scaffolds or extensions would ensure every student can access the task while still being challenged? Approaching AI suggestions with this kind of critical lens helps keep the focus on *why* we design in certain ways, not just on the tasks themselves, and I would argue it helps prevent the erosion our friends at MIT are warning us about.

This reflective step is where the magic of UDL really happens. Just as we encourage students to build on their strengths and work toward their best learning, we can do the same by treating AI as a starting point. From there, we make intentional, evidence-based decisions that build on what's working and tailor it to our specific students, context, and learning goals.

When we do this well, we're not just "following the robot's lead" or replacing our expertise with AI's output. We're practicing the same kind of balanced thinking we want students to develop, holding tight to the learning goal while staying open to flexible ways to reach it. So yes—absolutely embrace AI, or any other promising tools that come along, not only as you unpack your goals but as you design your learning environment. But never lose sight of your own brilliance, your expertise, and your love of the students in front of you. Those are the real drivers of great teaching. That balance—knowing exactly *what* learners must achieve while inviting multiple ways for getting there—is the heart of UDL.

Whether we're choosing materials, planning learning activities, or even using AI to generate ideas, the key is keeping the learning goal crystal clear while being open to flexible pathways. Dr. David Rose, the founder of Universal Design for Learning, put it this way:

> Clear goals for learning guide every curriculum consideration. To engage students and enable them to evaluate their own progress, we need to express learning goals, offer optional paths for achieving the goals, convey criteria for success, and build explicit ties to students' lives. Fuzzy goals confuse teachers and learners alike and risk unnecessary failure.[13]

That's where the challenge comes in. Real classrooms are messy, and sometimes we take multiple standards and combine the *what* and the *how*. That can make it hard to know exactly what you're assessing and where to give students flexibility. In practice, this means we have to be intentional about how we pair our goals with the ways students can meet them, and we must avoid muddying the waters by assessing too many skills at once.

As an English teacher, I often combined content and method standards. For example, I would select a text and ask students to "analyze how particular elements of a story or drama interact (e.g., how setting shapes the characters or plot)," and I would assign this as an essay. The focus of the instruction was on the elements of the plot, but students were also expected to master the standard: "Write informative/explanatory texts to examine a topic and convey ideas, concepts, and information through the selection, organization, and analysis of relevant content."

This is an example of double jeopardy. I am assessing both reading comprehension and writing, and it's difficult to untangle what students know from what they can do. Also, it's important to consider the instructional focus. Is the lesson focused on reading

13 Tracey E. Hall, Anne Meyer, and David H. Rose, eds., *Universal Design for Learning in the Classroom: Practical Applications* (Guilford Press, 2012), 94.

comprehension or writing? If it's truly both, then it would make sense to chunk the lesson into two parts.

Breaking it apart allows you to design with much greater clarity. It also creates a natural opening to bring AI in as a supportive tool, helping you design assessments and rubrics that keep the focus firmly on the goal.

In the first lesson, I could provide options for students to learn more about how setting shapes plot. This may include inquiry tasks, small-group instruction, and/or access to high-quality instructional materials on plot development. Next, I could design numerous opportunities for students to access a short, profound text. I could make hard copies available, encourage students to access the text digitally, or have them work in small groups with one person reading aloud or everyone taking turns. As students read, I could offer options to make their thinking visible as they analyze how the text's setting shapes the plot. This analysis could take many forms: a written analysis, a multimedia analysis (video or audio), or a short presentation. A simple rubric would help determine whether students have met the content standard. AI is great at creating these rubrics. Take the target standard in this lesson and the following prompt:

> You are my teaching assistant. Create a three-point holistic, asset-based rubric based on this seventh-grade standard: "Analyze how particular elements of a story or drama interact (e.g., how setting shapes the characters or plot)."

Within five seconds, I had the following:

Table 5.1: Holistic Rubric: Analyzing How Story Elements Interact (Grade 7, Asset-Based)

Level	Descriptor
3: Thorough and Insightful	Clearly and convincingly explains how two or more elements (e.g., setting, characters, plot) influence one another. Uses precise, relevant evidence to illustrate these connections and shows sophisticated reasoning about how the interactions shape the overall meaning of the story or drama.
2: Developing	Describes meaningful links between elements with generally accurate reasoning. Cites appropriate textual evidence, though some ideas could be elaborated further. Demonstrates a solid grasp of how interactions contribute to the story and is ready to deepen analysis with more specific details or nuance.
1: Emerging	Identifies key story elements and begins to explore how they might connect. Provides at least one example from the text and shows a growing awareness of how setting, characters, or plot can influence one another. Ready to build by adding more precise explanations and additional evidence.

Note how I prompted my robot friend. First, I gave it a persona (my teaching assistant); next, I shared the type of rubric I wanted (holistic, rather than analytic or single-point); and finally, I shared the exact language of the standard to ensure I was focused on content-relevant factors. I also prompted to ensure the rubric is asset-based, as many rubrics generated by both humans and AI will use deficit-based language. In a deficit-based rubric, "emerging" would read something like this: "Mentions story elements but offers limited or unclear explanations of their interaction. References to the text are minimal, inaccurate, or missing. Reasoning is superficial, showing little understanding of how the elements affect the narrative."

In many ways, they are saying the same thing, but as a teaching tool, I prefer the asset-based language in a rubric. This is where your professional judgment meets AI's efficiency; the tool can give you a starting point, but only you can ensure it aligns with the UDL commitment to high expectations and strengths-based feedback. Now, maybe the rubric above isn't perfect, but it's a solid draft we can refine to align with our purpose.

Using the rubric above, some students might produce writing, but I would not be assessing its quality, as that was not the focus of my instruction. That said, this kind of task could absolutely become part of the writing process if my ultimate goal were to have students share their analysis in a written product. If I were chunking the lesson, I'd treat this as a formative assessment during the pre-writing stage, a chance to check for content understanding before students start organizing their thoughts into a draft. The grade would reflect mastery of the reading standard, and once that content was mastered, we could transition into writing instruction.

If the goal shifts to assessing writing, then my instructional design needs to shift, too. That means modeling writing explicitly, using exemplars, providing graphic organizers, offering flexible ways to structure a piece, holding writing conferences—the whole shebang. I can write something quickly when I just need to explain what I understand, but if I know my writing will be assessed, that's not a sit-down-and-bust-it-out kind of moment. Great writing should never be treated as an event. It's a process: pre-writing, drafting, revising, editing, and publishing. If writing is the goal, students need instruction that honors that process, along with the time and tools to get there.

The Paradox of Choice

From the example above, you can see that universal design and firm goals and flexible means are about purpose and intentionality. Clarity gets us halfway there. The next step is designing the right amount of choice so that students are empowered, not overwhelmed. Even with a strong goal and thoughtfully designed options, the number of choices we offer matters. Too few options can limit access; too many can overwhelm and distract from the learning. Striking that balance is where the paradox of choice comes in.

Psychologist Barry Schwartz, who's done extensive research on decision-making and has a famous TED Talk on the topic, explains that while some choice is good, more choice isn't always better. He describes a spectrum of decision-making. On one end are the maximizers, who work really hard to make the best possible choice in every situation. On the other end are the satisficers, who are content with a choice that meets their needs, even if it's not perfect. Schwartz found that maximizers often experience more stress, more regret, and more second-guessing because they're so focused on finding the best option that it can prevent them from starting at all.[14]

Now think about how that plays out in a classroom with firm goals and flexible means. Let's say you give students a choice board. Some learners will pick the first option that aligns with their strengths and needs and get right to work. Others, especially maximizers, might become overwhelmed or anxious, unsure which option is "best," and they'll worry about making the wrong decision. This is why designing flexible means isn't just about variety; it's also about clarity and scaffolding.

I learned this lesson the hard way. When I was teaching seventh-grade English, I had a brilliant student, whom I will call Carla, who was very literal. She reminded me of the children's book

14 Barry Schwartz, "The Tyranny of Choice," *Scientific American* 290, no. 4 (April 2004): 70–75, https://doi.org/10.1038/scientificamerican0404-70.

character Amelia Bedelia, a cheerful housekeeper whose literal mind takes every instruction at face value. In one book, she is told to "draw the drapes," and she grabs paper and a pencil to create a work of art. In another, she has to "dress the turkey," and I'm sure you can guess how that turns out.

One day, I thought I was being clever by asking students to review some local take-out menus and then argue whose menu was the best. It was meant to be an activator, something that would take five minutes. Most students picked a place they liked and justified their choice with a quick explanation like "This one has roasted turkey, not deli slices." But Carla? She froze. She told me she couldn't possibly complete the task unless she had tasted food from every restaurant on the list. When I told her to just pick a place with a good menu, she pushed back. "You said best," she reminded me, wide-eyed and sincere. "I don't want to lie." Goodness, did I learn my lesson.

That moment changed how I framed every choice going forward. I had unintentionally forced Carla into the role of a maximizer with my wording. What I meant to offer was low-stakes engagement. What I actually did was introduce stress and cognitive overload for a student who needed more support in navigating options. Carla taught me that when we offer choice, we also have to teach students how to make choices, and we need to create space where "good enough" really is good enough. That day also made me rethink not just how I word options but how I model decision-making as part of learning.

So, how can we design more intentionally for learner agency within the structure of firm goals? First, be thoughtful about the number of options you offer. Schwartz recommends focusing on a small number of high-quality choices. Stick to between two and four. Then, create space for exploration. Encourage students to try something out, not to find the perfect match but to see what helps them learn. Instead of asking which strategy is "best," ask them, "Which one do you want to try first?" and "How will you know if it's helping you learn?" Let them know they can change course. This will help to shift the culture from perfection to progress and reflection.

Of course, teachers can only keep goals firm and the means flexible if the larger system reinforces that clarity. This is where leadership makes all the difference.

LEADERSHIP LENS

Firm goals only work if leaders reinforce them at the system level. When the message from leadership is inconsistent—"Hold all students to high standards" one day and "Just get them through the material" the next—teachers understandably default to what feels doable in the moment. Inconsistency creates anxiety, and anxiety leads to narrowing instruction rather than elevating it.

As leaders, our role is to name, protect, and reinforce the goals that matter most. That means being explicit about the non-negotiable outcomes students are expected to reach and equally explicit about where educators have professional autonomy. The clarity is the support. When people know which parts are firm and which are flexible, they are more confident in designing innovative, responsive instruction.

In practice, here's what this looks like:

- Begin every coaching conversation, PLC meeting, and planning session with the goal, not the task.
- Ask, "What is the learning students must walk away with?" before discussing strategies or materials.
- Review lesson plans by first looking for clarity of success criteria, then examining how flexibility is built in to get there.
- Celebrate when teachers take risks that align with the goal—even when the product isn't perfect yet.

This shift moves the culture from "How will you teach it?" to "How will you ensure students learn it?" It communicates that we value thinking and transfer, not just task completion.

Your Move: Clarity First, Flexibility Second

Think about a common learning goal or standard you teach. Now, reflect on how you've traditionally had students demonstrate mastery of that goal.

- What is the firm goal? Is it a content or method goal? How do you know?
- What are the flexible means you currently offer, or what flexible means could you offer?
- Can you identify one method goal that you've inadvertently tied to a content goal in your past teaching? What might it look like to untangle them and offer more flexible pathways for both?
- Consider the paradox of choice. How might you adjust the number or presentation of options you offer to ensure students are empowered, not overwhelmed, by choice?

Up Next

In this chapter, we journeyed from embracing the power of firm goals to intentionally designing flexible means. But simply offering choices isn't enough; true universal design empowers students to navigate those choices effectively and advocate for their own learning needs. In chapter 6, we'll dive into how to cultivate students' ability to intentionally shape their own learning experiences, building essential executive function skills that transform options into informed choices and self-directed learning.

CHAPTER 6

Planning for Learner Agency

When I (May or May Not Have) Flown to the Wrong City

Early in my career, I was invited to present at Pleasant Valley Unified School District. This was a big deal, one of my first out-of-state speaking gigs. I'd spent most of my career in districts named after towns (you know, places like Chelmsford and Groton-Dunstable), so when someone from Pleasant Valley asked if I needed the address for the central office, I smiled confidently and said, "Nope, I'm totally fine. I'll look it up."

Spoiler alert: I was not fine. I confidently booked a flight to Pleasant Valley, CA, which, for the record, is up near Chico, in Northern California. The *actual* Pleasant Valley Unified School District? It's in Camarillo, in Southern California. They're roughly four hundred miles apart.

At the time, I was still working as an assistant superintendent. I put in a full day at the office, raced to Logan Airport for a 7:00 p.m. flight, and landed in NorCal around 10:00 p.m. Pacific time, completely wiped but feeling good about my planning. I mean, my slides were ready to roll! That is, until I finally typed in the district office address to check for morning traffic and saw that my destination was in Camarillo, not anywhere near where I had just landed.

There was a brief moment (OK, an extended moment) where I considered crawling into the back seat and pretending my flight had been canceled. I may have cried. I definitely cursed my neurodivergent brain for thinking "I'll just look it up" was a solid strategy. I also briefly imagined texting the organizers something like "Funny story . . ." and then tossing my phone into a lake.

But then, something clicked. Agency. I took a breath. I assessed my options:

1. Try to catch another flight (nope, too late).
2. Drive all night (not desirable at all, but possible).
3. Sit in the Marriott parking lot and wallow in self-pity (tempting).

I chose option two. I downloaded *There There* by Tommy Orange (highly recommend), grabbed an iced coffee the size of my head, and set off into the night, grateful for audiobooks, caffeine, and an open window.

That trip sticks with me because it's a perfect metaphor for agency, the messy, real-life kind. The kind where you make a mistake, take ownership, assess your options, and move forward, not because someone told you to but because you believe in the work and you're committed to the goal. That's the version of agency I want to explore in this chapter: not just student choice but self-direction, informed decision-making, and ownership of the learning journey, even when it's a hot mess of your own doing.

Unpacking Agency

Learner agency is grounded in the idea that students have the capacity to shape their own learning. UDL's focus on agency builds on the research of Albert Bandura, who is basically the grandfather of the concept. He defined human agency as the ability to intentionally influence one's own life and learning, and he broke it down into four key parts:[15]

1. **Intentionality:** having a plan and taking purposeful action
2. **Forethought:** setting goals and anticipating possible outcomes
3. **Self-reactiveness:** staying motivated and adjusting your behavior along the way
4. **Self-reflectiveness:** thinking critically about what's working and what's not

Looking back, I checked all four of Bandura's boxes on my accidental detour through central California, whether I meant to or not. I had intentionality (I was determined to get to that district, even if I was in the wrong part of the state), forethought (once I realized the mistake, I made a new plan and figured out what it would take to get there by morning), self-reactiveness (I adjusted my behavior in real time), and self-reflectiveness (oh, there was reflection . . . lots of it, somewhere between hour three and hour six of that drive, where I vowed to always ask for an address). Agency is not about doing things perfectly. It's about moving forward with purpose, even when things don't go the way you expected.

When we talk about building agency, we're not just offering students more choices and hoping for the best. We're helping them develop the skills and confidence to make meaningful decisions,

15 Albert Bandura, "Human Agency in Social Cognitive Theory," *American Psychologist* 44, no. 9 (1989): 1175–1184, https://doi.org/10.1037/0003-066X.44.9.1175.

create strategies, reflect, and grow as learners. To build learner agency, we have to design for learner agency. So what does that kind of design actually look like when it's done well? Let's start with one of the most common ways teachers introduce flexibility, which is through content, process, and product choices:

- **Content choices** allow students to make decisions about what they learn. Students can pursue learning through a lens of interest.
- **Process choices** invite students to decide how they do something. Students decide how to complete a task given their strengths and learning preferences.
- **Product choices** give students meaningful options for how they communicate or demonstrate their learning.

When we talk about building agency, we're not just offering students more choices and hoping for the best. We're helping them develop the skills and confidence to make meaningful decisions, create strategies, reflect, and grow as learners.

Let's examine all three in an elementary science lesson aligned to this Next Generation Science Standard: "Construct an argument that some animals form groups that help members survive."

The teacher could offer content options by allowing students to choose their animal group. Students could choose from numerous options to learn about the animal group they selected. Some students may research videos, while others borrow books from the library or use an online research tool to learn. Finally, students could choose how to present their argument. Some students may write an argument, while others may create a multimedia presentation or a short video.

This is a super flexible lesson, but it may overwhelm some students or lead others to try to figure out the "easiest" option. Or students may simply choose pathways that don't serve them as learners because they want to pick what their friends pick. All these barriers result from lagging skills, which prevent students from building agency. In looking at the four components of agency, imagine if the lesson above included the following elements.

1. Intentionality

Before students dive into research, ask them to complete a quick planning organizer. There could be numerous prompts, and students could have flexible options for how they respond (e.g., written notes, voice recordings, graphic organizers, or peer discussions). Here are some sample prompts:

- What animal group are you choosing and why?
- What do you already know about this animal?
- How do you plan to learn more? (Video, book, research tool, interview, etc.) Why do you think this strategy will be an effective way for you to learn more about your animal group?

This step builds clarity and purpose. Students aren't just choosing randomly; they're setting themselves up for focused exploration.

2. Forethought

Once students have activated their background knowledge and begun planning, embed a short goal-setting routine that helps them anticipate their own needs and set realistic expectations. This could be done using a digital form, a sticky-note goal wall, or a short journal entry. Here are some sample sentence starters:

- By the end of this week, I want to . . .
- If I get stuck, I'll try . . .
- One way I'll know I'm making progress is . . .

You might also ask students to review the available product options and reflect on which one will help them share their thinking clearly. Support this with simple reflection questions:

- Which option feels exciting to you? Why?
- Which option might be more challenging?
- Do you feel ready to take on that challenge, or do you need more practice first?

This helps students start to think ahead, not just about what they want to do but about why it matters and what it will take to be successful.

3. Self-Reactiveness

Build in multiple check-ins during the research and creation phases, allowing students to pause and reflect on their progress. These don't need to be long. You might provide a quick reflection template that students complete individually in writing, with a partner, or via a short video. Here are some possible prompts:

- How's it going so far? (Have them use an emoji and/or write one to two sentences.)
- If I had to assess myself right now on the product rubric, where would I be and why?
- Is my strategy effective, or do I need to make a change?

Encourage students to view these pauses as part of the process. If things aren't going well, normalize the idea that learners pivot. That's how they grow.

4. Self-Reflectiveness

After completing their project, students can engage in a short reflection on lessons learned about both the content and the learning process. This is key for helping them build a deeper understanding of what works for them and what doesn't. Here are some sample prompts:

- What went well?
- What would you do differently next time?
- What did you learn about yourself as a learner?

To keep it accessible, allow students to choose how they reflect: through a voice note, a short paragraph, a comic strip, or even a reflection conversation with you as a teacher. The format matters far less than the insight. The goal is for students to leave the experience not just knowing more about animal behavior but also knowing more about *themselves* as learners. That's how agency grows.

Research supports the value of this type of student reflection in education. Daily reflection helps students internalize what they've learned, recognize their strengths and weaknesses, and develop metacognitive skills. In his groundbreaking study *Visible Learning*, John Hattie states that reflection has an effect size of 0.79, making it a powerful tool for learning that can result in two years of academic growth—so it's incredibly worthwhile to build this into your practice.[16] To help students reflect consistently and effectively, consider implementing the following strategies in your learning environment.

Opening and Closing Routines

Start and end each class with routines that prompt reflection and visual thinking. For example, after you share the day's learning

16 John Hattie, "Hattie Ranking: Influences on Student Achievement," *Visible Learning*, accessed January 12, 2026, https://visible-learning.org/hattie-ranking-influences-effect-sizes-learning-achievement/.

objective, prompt students with a question like "What do you hope to learn today?" and end with "What was the most important thing you learned today?" These routines encourage students to set goals and reflect on their progress. As with all things UDL, provide options and choices for students to reflect. If you don't feel like you can carve out time for these reflections every day, commit to building a habit of completing them once a week. For example, you can use the last ten minutes of class on Friday like this: Ask students to review their notes from the week, have them log in to check their grades, and then have them choose from a short list of reflection questions. With younger students, replace logging in to grades with reviewing a folder or portfolio of their work. Then guide them to highlight something they are proud of and identify one thing they want to improve. Finally, have them choose from a few visual or sentence-starter reflection prompts such as "This week I learned . . ." or "One thing that was tricky for me was . . ." or "Next week I want to try . . ."

Exam Wrapper Questions

In addition to daily routines, you can embed reflection directly into assessments. I love using the exam wrapper for this; it's a simple but powerful tool that surrounds an assessment with reflection. Before students take a quiz or complete a project, they respond to one or two questions about how they prepared, what strategies they used, or how confident they feel. After they get their graded assessment back, they revisit those reflections and respond to follow-up questions about what worked, what didn't, and what they'd do differently next time.

The real value of an exam wrapper is helping students connect the dots between the choices they make while learning and the outcomes they experience. It gives them a structure to reflect on their learning process and build metacognitive awareness.

To try this in your own classroom, start by brainstorming a short list of questions students could answer before and after any assessment. In *The Shift to Student-Led*, Catlin Tucker[17] and I created sample exam wrapper questions that you can pull from or adapt to fit your content and goals (table 6.1). Think about which questions might help your students better understand how they learn, how they prepare, and how they can improve, and then build those into your regular assessment routines.

Table 6.1: Exam Wrapper Reflection Prompts

Before the Assessment	After the Assessment
• How prepared do you feel to take this formative assessment? • What are the learning experiences we have had in this class that relate to the focus of this assessment? • Before you share what you know, what areas are you feeling confident in? • Before you share what you know, what specific concepts or skills are you feeling unsure of? • What did you do to prepare for this assessment? How helpful were these strategies?	• If you struggled to share what you have learned, what was the main reason why? • What questions do you still have after reviewing the results of this assessment? • Did anything surprise you as you reviewed your results? • Did you notice growth or improvement in any areas? • What are your next steps in terms of acting on the results of this assessment?

For younger students, exam wrappers can be adapted by simplifying the language, using sentence starters, and incorporating visuals or icons. Before the assessment, students might circle a face to show how ready they feel, complete the sentence "One thing I know I can do well on this is . . ." or choose one thing they want to work extra hard on. They can also identify how they prepared by selecting from options such as practicing flash cards, reading notes, or working

17 Catlin R. Tucker and Katie Novak, *The Shift to Student-Led: Reimagining Classroom Workflows with UDL and Blended Learning* (Impress, 2022).

with a partner. After the assessment, they might again circle a face to show how they feel about their work, share one thing they are proud of, name something they want to improve, and choose a new strategy to try next time. By making the process concrete, visual, and choice-based, even young learners can reflect on their preparation, performance, and next steps in ways that build metacognitive skills.

Regular Check-Ins

To support agency, it's also valuable to have regular check-ins with students to talk about their progress, challenges, and reflections. These can be one-on-one conversations or small-group discussions in which students take the lead in sharing how things are going and what support they need. You could schedule these check-ins monthly to establish a consistent routine in your learning environment.

You'll get more bang for your buck when these conversations include student-led progress updates. Instead of always guiding the conversation, give students a few minutes to prepare so they can reflect, share evidence of their learning, and articulate their goals. As part of the check-in, invite students to create a short artifact that captures the discussion. This could be a quick email or note home to the adults in their lives, a sixty-second video update, or a written summary that can inform your report card comments. When students are responsible for documenting their own progress, they build metacognitive awareness. It also creates a bridge to family engagement, as updates come directly from the student with your support.

This is also a great strategy when working with our youngest learners. My five-year-old nephew, Lawson, attends speech therapy every week. He's been going for a couple of years now, and while progress takes time, the growth is clear. Looking at his data from when he started at age two to now, you can see remarkable gains in his speech skills. Week to week, the changes are subtle, but they are captured in a way that makes them visible. After each session, Lawson fills out a simple "A Note from Your Speech Star" form side by side with his teacher. On a recent sheet, he recorded that he worked on /s/ blends and practiced a "give a clue" clear speech strategy. He circled the "Awesome!!!" face to show how he felt about his progress and noted that he's still working on the "st" sound in words like *stop*. Then his speech teacher highlighted that he had mastered a previously tricky word, *spoon*. This little artifact (figure 6.1) was sent home so his parents could celebrate his successes and see exactly what he's working toward. It's quick, student driven, and a perfect example of how documenting progress can build ownership and keep families connected to learning.

The real power is that students aren't just participating in reflection; they're leading it. Reflection isn't an add-on for when there's extra time. It's a core skill that builds the agency students need to take ownership of their learning.

LEADERSHIP LENS

If we want students to reflect in meaningful ways, we need to model that same expectation with educators. Reflection shouldn't just be something we encourage teachers to do with students; it should be a regular part of how we support, coach, and grow with our teams, and we should model it ourselves.

Ask yourself these questions:

- When do teachers have dedicated time to reflect on what's working and what needs adjustment in their classrooms?
- How do our coaching conversations and leadership meetings make space for honest reflection?
- How do we model reflection ourselves after PD sessions, classroom walk-throughs, or faculty meetings?

When we as leaders create space for teacher reflection and treat it as essential, not optional, it's far more likely to show up in classrooms. And when it does, it creates a powerful ripple effect: better decisions, deeper learning, and stronger ownership at every level.

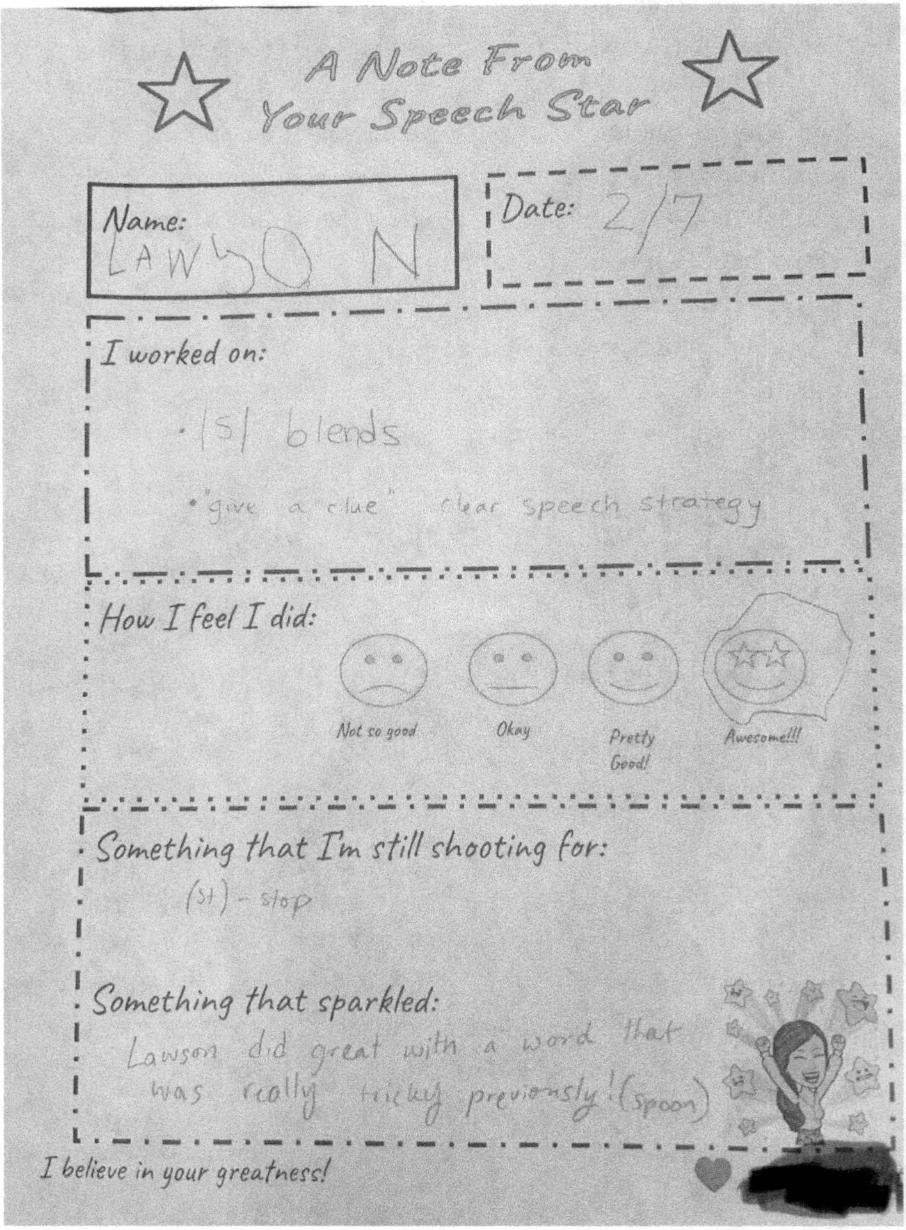

A Note From Your Speech Star

Name: LAWSON

Date: 2/7

I worked on:

- /s/ blends
- "give a clue" clear speech strategy

How I feel I did:

Not so good | Okay | Pretty Good! | Awesome!!!

Something that I'm still shooting for:

(st) - stop

Something that sparkled:

Lawson did great with a word that was really tricky previously! (spoon)

I believe in your greatness!

Figure 6.1: Lawson's Speech Reflection

Skills for the Future

Learner agency isn't just helpful in school. It's what students will need to thrive beyond it. According to the World Economic Forum *Future of Jobs Report 2025*,[18] some of the top skills on the rise are self-awareness, creative thinking, flexibility and agility, curiosity, and lifelong learning. These aren't soft skills. They're life skills, and they grow when students have regular opportunities to make decisions, reflect on outcomes, and choose their pathways as they move forward.

We know these skills matter. The challenge is how to teach and measure them in ways that are developmentally appropriate and truly useful. That's where the BEST *Self-Direction Toolkit*[19] comes in. It was developed by the Building Essential Skills Today (BEST) Research-Practice Partnership, a collaboration among teachers, school leaders, researchers, and numerous organizations, and it was created to elevate how schools teach and assess self-direction through a developmental lens. I *love* sharing these rubrics with educators because they show how self-direction and learner agency develop over time.

Let's examine the K–2 rubric, which includes descriptors for self-awareness, initiative and ownership, goal-setting and planning, engaging and managing, and monitoring and adapting (table 6.2).

18 World Economic Forum, *Future of Jobs Report 2025*, January 2025, https://reports.weforum.org/docs/WEF_Future_of_Jobs_Report_2025.pdf.

19 BEST Research-Practice Partnership, *Self-Direction Toolkit: Version 1.0*. Accessed January 12, 2026, https://www.best-future.org/wp-content/uploads/2020/10/BEST%20Self-Direction%20Toolkit-v1.pdf.

Table 6.2: BEST Self-Direction K–2 Rubric

Level	Self-Awareness	Initiative and Ownership	Goal Setting and Planning	Engaging and Managing	Monitoring and Adapting
Emerging	I can identify the tasks I'd like to work on, when I am given choices.	I can try new experiences to find out what might be interesting to me, with support.	I can follow a process my teacher showed me to identify steps or strategies that will help me meet a learning goal.	I can explain what I learned when I used a resource, or when I used a strategy guided by my teacher.	I can keep working on learning tasks with encouragement from others.
Developing	I can explain why I made a choice, describing my strengths, my interests, or why I am not interested in doing a task.	I can select and complete tasks I am interested in doing, with support from others.	I can explain how or why the strategy used at each step of a plan would help me complete a familiar task.	I can follow a process my teacher taught me to select the best resources or strategies needed to complete a specific task.	I can provide examples of how I changed my approach or made the quality of my work better, when prompted.
Applying	I can describe how I used my strengths to complete a learning task.	I can ask for help or ask relevant questions that help me keep working to complete a task.	I can follow a process my teacher taught me to plan the steps and strategies needed to complete a new task.	I can follow a process using checkpoints identified by my teacher or my peers to make progress toward completing multistep tasks.	I can identify the strategies that worked well and explain why I think they worked.
Extending	I can compare examples of my past and present work to show how I used my strengths to make progress.	I can work with my peers to develop a new learning task or broaden an existing task to make it more interesting to us.	I can use feedback from others to decide if my plan will work and make changes to improve my plan.	I can describe how I tried different strategies to find the best one that worked the best when completing a task.	I can tell how and why I might make changes next time to improve the quality of my work.

As you can see from the rubric, the earliest stages of self-direction and agency require opportunities for choice, even if those choices are not yet informed or strategic. Young learners are often driven by interest rather than by a clear connection to their strengths or goals. Our role is to design experiences where they can safely make choices, reflect on them, and begin to see how those choices influence the quality and clarity of their work. Within a UDL framework, we anticipate these emerging skills and embed supports, scaffolded reflection, modeling, and feedback to help students learn from the decisions they make. Over time, these supports intentionally move students from *emerging* toward *extending* on the rubric, with agency developing through guided practice.

So, what does that look like?

Let's start in kindergarten. Imagine students are working on this standard: "With prompting and support, retell familiar stories, including key details, and demonstrate understanding of their central message or lesson." After reading *The Little Red Hen* together several times (using a mix of read-alouds, picture walks, and acting out the story), students are invited to retell the story and share what they think the lesson is.

Rather than requiring everyone to use the same format, you offer multiple ways for students to show their understanding:

- Draw a series of pictures showing the beginning, middle, and end, and explain the story to a partner.
- Use puppets or props to act out the story while a peer or teacher records the retelling.
- Sequence printed story cards in order and record an audio retelling on a tablet.

The learning goal is the same for everyone: Clearly retell the story and explain its lesson. Each student chooses the story format that works best for them and, in some cases, a partner to collaborate with.

After sharing, students engage in scaffolded reflection:

- **Self-awareness:** Why did you choose this way to retell the story?

"I picked _______ because . . ."

- **Monitoring and adapting:** What might you change or add next time to make your retelling clearer?

"Next time, I will . . ."

You could also model your own thinking to make the process visible:

> I picked the puppets because I like moving the characters while I tell the story. Moving the puppets helps me remember the order of the events because I can put them in the spots where they go in the story. See how I lined them up here? First the hen, then the duck, then the cat? That helps me keep track. I made sure to show how the hen asked for help three times because I think that is the most important part of the story. It shows that the animals kept saying no. Next time, I might add more about what happened after the bread was ready so my audience knows why the other animals didn't get any. I could even add a scene right here [move puppets] where they ask for bread and she says no.

In this example, students are exercising initiative and ownership by selecting their format, and they're demonstrating self-awareness by explaining why they chose it. They practice engaging and managing as they prepare and share their retelling, and they begin developing monitoring and adapting skills as they identify changes they could make for next time. With ongoing opportunities like this, supported by intentional reflection prompts, students begin to see themselves as active, capable learners. That's agency in its earliest form.

Now zoom forward a few years.

As a chemistry teacher, you may require students to write reports to share their findings from labs. At a scientific conference, some researchers share their findings in traditional lab reports, which are often white papers, but other scientists present in poster sessions, on a panel, or through a visual scientific display. During the first four months of school, you might ask students to complete each of these four formats in low-stakes learning opportunities—a lab report, poster session, panel discussion, and visual presentation—so they gain experience with different communication methods. After each attempt, students reflect on their strengths in that medium, challenges they encountered, and strategies they want to work on next time. Only after students have had the chance to experience each format, see clear exemplars, and engage in peer review can they really begin to make informed choices.

These are also realistic choices. I present at numerous conferences each year and am often given the option to choose the format of the presentation I will submit. Sometimes there are options for mini-sessions, full-day workshops, or panels. Although my preference is usually a full-day workshop because it allows for the most meaningful connections, ongoing work, and opportunities for application, I am also familiar with the other formats. That's what we want for our students: to enable them to explore different pathways, build competence in several, and ultimately identify one that plays to their strengths while still having the versatility to adapt when needed.

And it's important to highlight that when we ask students to explore different mediums, each format needs to be flexible and universally designed. The first draft of a lab report can be typed or handwritten and supported with sentence frames, speech-to-text tools, and scaffolded graphic organizers. A poster session can be digital or physical and created on paper or with design software. A presentation can be live or recorded and involve an individual or a group. A visual presentation might be an infographic, a digital poster, or a short video explanation.

This approach ensures students are exploring not only different formats but also different ways of engaging with those formats. This helps them build fluency, confidence, and the skills to make informed decisions. But here's the thing: Most students won't naturally say, "Let me reflect on my growth in visual presentation versus academic writing." And that's OK. To make reflection visible, manageable, and meaningful, build in scaffolds that guide students through the process. Here are ways you can achieve this:

- Model each format using exemplars and think-alouds so students can see what a strong product looks like and hear the reasoning behind specific choices.
- Provide peer feedback protocols that are clear, kind, and specific, and give students time to practice using them.
- Offer sentence stems such as "One thing I struggled with was . . ." or "I felt confident when . . ." to help students reflect in concrete, specific ways.
- Create a simple reflection checklist or template after each experience so students can quickly capture their strengths, challenges, and next steps.

It also means normalizing struggle and reminding students that this isn't about getting it "right" the first time. We can't expect students to demonstrate agency if we haven't helped them develop the tools to reflect, compare, and make purposeful choices.

Your Move: Be an Agent of Agency

Throughout this chapter, you learned that agency is about the inherent messiness of learning and the need for trial and error, consistent and ongoing reflection, and figuring out what works best on each individual's journey. And just like students, we grow when we reflect. Before moving on to the next chapter, take a moment to consider these questions to help your own growth:

- When have students struggled to make meaningful choices? What structures or scaffolds may have been missing?
- Where have I seen students thrive because they had time to reflect, revise, or make decisions about their learning?
- What opportunities do I already offer for student agency? How are students responding?
- Where could I build in one new opportunity for reflection or intentional decision-making this month? (Now, try it!)

Up Next

OK, so you're at least partly on board with UDL if you've read this far. But let's be honest: Many educators don't have a blank slate. They're asked to "teach with fidelity" to high-quality instructional materials and prepare students for inflexible standardized tests. At the same time, they're asked to implement UDL, which may seem in conflict. So, how do we embrace the UDL mindset when we face these very real conditions? In the next part of this book, we'll dig into how you can leverage the UDL framework even when using adopted curriculum materials or preparing students for the realities of standardized testing. Worry not—I've got you.

PART 3

Making It Work in the Real World

CHAPTER 7

High-Quality Instructional Materials Meet UDL

Clinically Proven . . . If You Actually Follow the Directions

A few years ago, my college roommate, Sarah, became passionate about clean beauty. One day, she told me about a new vitamin C serum her company had launched. The evidence was fabulous—dare I say "clinically proven." After eight weeks of use, 100 percent of the thirty-two subjects said their skin looked brighter. Ninety-four percent said the serum had reduced dark spots. I mean, c'mon. It sounded like magic. Given such glowing results, I opted in immediately and used the serum faithfully for eight weeks. Or so I thought. At the end, I used a magnification mirror, took side-by-side photos . . . and saw nothing. No glow. No fading spots. Nada.

When I complained to Sarah, she asked, "Did you use it like you were supposed to?" I rolled my eyes. How hard is it to apply serum in the morning? But when I actually read the instructions on the back of the bottle, I realized I had skipped a few crucial steps. If I were following the regimen exactly as in the clinical trial, I would have cleansed, toned, applied "my regimen's serum" (note: I had no regimen), then applied the magic serum, then lotion. My real morning routine? Wake up, run, shower, lotion with sunscreen, and serum. I washed my face at night, rinsed it in the morning, and called it good.

Sarah laughed and said, "You can't say it doesn't work if you didn't use it the way it was supposed to be used."

Ah, what a perfect analogy for education.

The Fidelity Connection

Just as my serum results had more to do with my use than with the product itself, our classroom results depend on whether we are implementing the program as designed. In schools, we often adopt high-quality instructional programs with strong evidence of effectiveness. But if we don't take the time to unpack and internalize the curriculum, or (logistically speaking) we can't follow the methodology used in the research, we can't expect the same results. Fidelity to high-quality instructional materials (HQIM) doesn't mean teaching like a robot. It means understanding the methodology, honoring the intent of the program, and making intentional, consistent decisions so all learners can access and engage with the content.

Fidelity to high-quality instructional materials (HQIM) doesn't mean teaching like a robot. It means understanding the methodology, honoring the intent of the program, and making intentional, consistent decisions so all learners can access and engage with the content.

That's easier said than done. Class periods are different lengths, student needs vary, and resources don't always match what was available in the research context. When those gaps happen, we improvise, and that can lead to program drift, where small changes accumulate until we are no longer delivering the same thing that was studied. And that's when we often end up thinking, "It doesn't work." This brings us to the other big piece: understanding what *evidence based* really means and why matching the research to your own context matters.

When "Evidence Based" Isn't a Magic Wand

If you have adopted instructional materials, I hope they're evidence based, meaning high-quality studies show students achieved positive outcomes using them. But not all evidence is created equal. *Evidence based* can mean a lot of things. It could mean a large experimental study with random assignment, a smaller quasi-experimental study, or even a correlational study that only shows a relationship.

The key question is this: How closely do the study's participants, conditions, and resources match yours? If the original research involved longer instructional blocks, very different students, or more planning time than you have, the same results are unlikely without intentional adaptation. To get similar outcomes, we need to understand and match the methodology used in the research. That means asking these questions:

- How much instructional time was allocated for each lesson or unit?
- What training and ongoing support did teachers receive before and during implementation?
- How were materials used, including the sequence, pace, grouping structures, and differentiation?
- What supplemental tools or scaffolds were built into the delivery?

If the study's conditions don't match ours, we simply cannot assume the same outcomes.

I was working with a group of educators in Nebraska who were told to implement a math program "with fidelity." I was familiar with the program and had seen it work in other districts, so I asked what was making it so challenging. They explained that they had forty-eight-minute periods, but the program's lessons were designed for seventy minutes.

"Wait," I said. "You do realize it's literally impossible to use that program with fidelity when you're twenty-two minutes short?"

"But our leaders say we have to," they replied.

"But you can't," I insisted.

We became besties after that. The bigger point is this: If you can't implement a program exactly as designed, you need a clear, standardized plan to adapt it—one that every teacher understands and has the training to use. And it must allow them to check whether it's actually working.

What Works, Wisconsin, a research team at the University of Wisconsin–Madison/Extension,[20] offers helpful guidance here: Decide together what you can keep, what you must change, and how you'll measure whether the adaptation works. I'll summarize these ideas below.

1. **What can we keep?** Identify the program's *essential components* that are most closely tied to its evidence of effectiveness. These might include specific instructional routines, the sequence in which skills are taught, or the way new concepts are introduced. Keep these consistent across classrooms so students receive the same high-leverage practices.

20 Cailin O'Connor et al., *Program Fidelity and Adaptation: Meeting Local Needs Without Compromising Program Effectiveness*, What Works, Wisconsin: Research to Practice Series no. 4 (University of Wisconsin-Madison and University of Wisconsin–Extension, 2007).

2. **What needs to change, and why?** Identify barriers that make it impossible to implement the program as intended. Is there insufficient instructional time? Are materials or assessments inaccessible to some students? Is required technology unavailable? Document both the barrier and the reason for the change so that the adaptation is purposeful.
3. **How will we know if it's still working?** Establish clear short-cycle measures (every two to four weeks) to monitor progress toward program goals. Use this data to determine whether the adaptation maintains or improves effectiveness. The goal is continuous improvement.

And here's the non-negotiable: Once you've standardized the adaptation, share the plan across the team. If every teacher adapts differently, you can't figure out what's actually working. Once you've either confirmed you can implement with fidelity or you've developed a standardized adaptation, you are ready for the next step, which is applying the UDL lens to ensure all students can access and engage with the learning. To see what this looks like in practice, let's consider a real example from a widely used literature-based English language arts curriculum.

The UDL Lens: An HQIM Example

I recently worked with a team tasked with implementing an HQIM program while integrating UDL. In their case, they were logistically able to implement the program with full fidelity, but, like many educators, they were worried that the program's structure would limit their ability to design for learner variability. When I reviewed a grade 3 lesson alongside them, I saw a fabulous amount of flexibility already built into the materials. The tip I gave to the teachers was simple: Highlight and explode the verbs.

In the program, lesson 1 asks students to "respond in writing" to questions like "How does reading make you feel?" And it offers the option to "draw how reading makes you feel." Already, there's flexibility, but we can take that even further. What does "writing" mean? Could it be pencil and paper? Sure. But could it also mean typing on a Chromebook, using speech-to-text, or using a sentence frame? You bet it does! And when the option is to "draw," could that be crayons? Yep. But it could also be a digital sketch tool or a collage from magazine clippings. Fidelity doesn't mean sameness. If the directions say "write or draw," your job is to make sure every student has a way to write or draw, even if their tools or formats look different.

Another verb that shows up all over the program is *read*. In lesson 1, the teacher is directed to read a short, profound text aloud to the whole class while students follow along, and that may be a non-negotiable first read. But the real opportunity for flexibility comes during rereads. After students have listened to the story once, they're invited to revisit it, noticing, wondering, and reflecting on questions like "What does reading mean to this character?" This is where the verb *read* can be exploded. Students might reread independently, in pairs, or in small groups. Some might follow along with a printed copy while the teacher reads it aloud again. Others could use a text-to-speech tool. The goal is to engage with the text, not to all decode at the same pace or in the same way. By keeping the first read consistent and opening up flexible pathways for rereading, teachers can honor both the curriculum *and* their students' needs.

Later in the lesson, students are prompted to discuss what they notice and wonder about the story using the think-pair-share routine. The verb here is *discuss*, but what does that actually look like? Students could turn and talk, yes, but there is so much potential for flexibility, especially in the *think* portion of the protocol. Some students may want to jot down a few ideas on a Post-it before talking, while others might use a digital tool to record a quick voice memo or type out their thoughts. Some might prefer to draw or annotate what they noticed before sharing it aloud. Then comes the *pair* and *share*—and even here, options matter. Some students may choose to sit on the floor, knee to knee, while others may prefer to stand and chat to help manage their energy. A few might want to use a talking piece to support turn-taking or to feel more confident when it's their turn. The goal is still meaningful peer discussion, grounded in the text. But exploding the verb allows students to access that goal in a way that works for them, and that's what inclusive design is all about.

That same flexibility applies when students are asked to reflect. At the end of the lesson, they're prompted to consider this question: "How does think-pair-share help you learn?" That's a beautiful moment for metacognition, and just like the other routines, it doesn't need to be one-size-fits-all. Some students may want to write a journal entry, but others might create a comic strip, record a short video or audio message, sketch a one-frame visual, or write a poem. They could respond individually, collaborate with a peer, or even share anonymously. The point is not *how* they reflect but that they *do* reflect. It's important that we value the many ways students can show their understanding, insight, and self-awareness.

Hopefully, you can see that exploding the verbs doesn't mean throwing out the curriculum. It means asking ourselves this: "What is the learning goal here, and how can more students get there with confidence and clarity?"

And this is a place where AI and your students can be helpful partners, too. If you copy a section of the teacher's guide (especially one with directions that include key verbs) into a prompt, you can ask the AI to list multiple ways to approach those verbs while still honoring the goal. For example, you might paste in "students respond in writing" and prompt, "Give me three different accessible options for how students could 'respond in writing' while keeping the same learning goal." AI will often surface possibilities you haven't yet considered, from digital tools to alternative formats. You can then refine these based on your expertise, students' needs, and your classroom context.

And you and the robots don't have to be the only ones doing this thinking. Inviting students into the process of exploding the verbs can build their agency and deepen their understanding of both the learning goal and the options available to them. For example, after introducing a task from the teacher's guide, you might say, "The directions say we will 'respond in writing.' What are some ways we could do that?" Students might suggest using speech-to-text, typing, creating a comic with captions, or using a graphic organizer before writing. This is just one example of how we can shift some of our planning workflows to our amazing learners.

My friend and colleague Catlin Tucker and I explored this idea in depth when we co-wrote *The Shift to Student-Led*. In that work, we found that when students are treated as co-designers of learning, the classroom transforms. They start seeing themselves as active partners in shaping how they learn and showing what they know, and we gain richer insight into how to remove barriers and extend challenges. This isn't about giving up control; it's about putting those babies to work, as they are so capable!

LEADERSHIP LENS

When schools adopt high-quality instructional materials, leaders have an opportunity to help teachers get the most out of them. Fidelity to the program ensures we're implementing the evidence-based practices as intended, while flexibility ensures every learner can access and engage with the content. The most effective leaders create clarity around the non-negotiables while also affirming teachers' professional judgment in making purposeful adaptations to meet learner variability.

Reflection questions for leaders:

- Have we clearly identified the essential components of our adopted materials so teachers can focus their energy on the parts that matter most?
- Have we provided time, space, and support for teachers to use the UDL Guidelines to design adaptations that remove barriers and strengthen alignment to standards?
- How do we celebrate examples of teachers making thoughtful, student-centered adaptations that maintain the integrity of the program while increasing access and engagement?

You might be thinking, "This would be great if I were teaching an adopted curriculum, but my context is different, and the content is fixed." Maybe you teach IB, AP, honors, dual enrollment, or a highly specialized course. But the truth is that the same principles apply.

Firm goals are not the problem. Whether the goal is meeting a district benchmark, preparing students for the IB Diploma Programme assessments, or ensuring they're ready for an AP exam, the content and rigor can remain intact while you embed flexibility in how students access, engage with, and express their learning.

Ask yourself these questions:

- How can I offer multiple ways for students to process complex texts, problems, or concepts?
- Can I integrate choice in the tools or resources students use to meet the goal?
- How can I vary collaboration structures so all students can contribute meaningfully?
- What scaffolds or supports could I proactively offer that will help more students reach the high bar?

The point is not to lower expectations. Rather, it is to open more pathways so every student has a fair opportunity to meet them. IB,

AP, and other rigorous programs already have firm, non-negotiable outcomes. UDL simply ensures that the road to those outcomes is accessible to a wider range of learners.

Your Move: Balance Fidelity with UDL

Think about your next lesson that includes an adopted resource, a routine you're asked to follow, or a moment of explicit instruction. Ask yourself these questions:

- What's one verb students are asked to do? (E.g., *read*, *write*, *discuss*, *reflect*, *analyze*.)
- Can you explode that verb and offer students more than one way to get there?
- Is there a predictable barrier that you can design for before it shows up?

As you learned in this chapter, you don't need to toss out or rewrite the curriculum. Start by choosing one verb and reimagine what flexibility might look like.

Up Next

Let's be honest: Even when we design inclusive, engaging, and rigorous instruction, there's still the looming pressure of state tests and benchmark assessments. How do we prepare students for those kinds of tasks, especially when they are rarely universally designed? In the next chapter, we focus on how students can be supported in showing what they know and can do on standardized assessment tasks, while maintaining the depth and integrity of strong instruction.

CHAPTER 8

Preparing for Standardized Assessments

Follow the Yellow Brick Road

When I was little, *The Wizard of Oz* was one of those movies I'd watch every single time it was on. I remember pulling up our piano bench so I could sit right in front of the television, my legs dangling and swinging back and forth as I sang along with Dorothy. The movie is a classic for a reason—the yellow brick road, the "lions and tigers and bears, oh my!," and that moment when the screen transitioned in the most magical way from black-and-white into Technicolor.

Fast-forward to my years in the classroom, and I realized something: Teaching feels a little like that jarring moment when one world becomes another. I would spend months leading students along universally designed paths of curiosity, creativity, and critical thinking. Then, the standardized testing window opened, and we were back in grainy black-and-white.

There is so much talk about meaningful tasks, authentic assessments, and deep learning, yet we are still serving the Wizard of

Standardized Tests, hidden behind the curtain, demanding we measure student success by rigid, outdated, one-size-fits-all methods. It feels like a bizarro-world version of *The Wizard of Oz*. I hear it all the time: "We'd love to implement UDL, but we have to prepare students for standardized tests." And here's the reality: Yes, we still have to prepare students for inaccessible tests. But that doesn't mean we have to use inaccessible practices to do it.

For a system that claims to measure college and career readiness, it's glaringly ironic how little standardized tests reflect the way professionals actually work in the real world. In my daily life, I use voice memos, speech-to-text, AI-powered tools, and multiple drafts before even considering showing my work to a colleague or editor. Nothing you read here is exactly like what I drafted, as I have had countless opportunities to share it with friends, colleagues, developmental editors, and copy editors to ensure it's ready for *you*. Yet we expect students to demonstrate what they know in a single, high-stakes setting, using tools that strip away the very supports they rely on in every other aspect of their lives.

And let's be honest. How many of us could sit down right now and take a high school physics or algebra exam (if you don't teach those subjects) under timed conditions without access to outside resources? Would we feel confident that a multiple-choice test could fully capture our intelligence, creativity, and problem-solving skills?

Until large-scale testing becomes more inclusive (there are small signs it's shifting), our job is twofold:

1. We must design learning experiences that are engaging, rigorous, and built on firm goals with flexible means, as we've been discussing throughout this book.
2. We have to explicitly teach students the skills and strategies that help them confidently navigate the current testing system without believing it's the only measure of their worth.

If we're not careful, test prep can send the wrong message: that learning is about compliance, not curiosity; that it's about getting the right answer, not thinking critically; and that the ultimate goal is scoring well rather than using knowledge to create, innovate, and succeed.

If we're not careful, test prep can send the wrong message: that learning is about compliance, not curiosity; that it's about getting the right answer, not thinking critically; and that the ultimate goal is scoring well rather than using knowledge to create, innovate, and succeed.

The good news? Change is coming. The College Board went fully digital with the SAT in 2024 and rolled out fully digital AP exams in 2025. The IB will begin piloting digital exams in the spring of 2026. Some assessments are beginning to incorporate more accessibility tools. And if we look at other fields, like voting, we see that large-scale systems can become more inclusive. If that system can evolve from exclusively in-person voting to mail-in ballots, early voting, and accommodations, testing can evolve too.

Standardized testing doesn't have to be the way it is. But as long as standardized tests remain a gatekeeper to college admissions, scholarships, and graduation, we have to equip students to succeed within the system, without compromising everything we know about great teaching and learning.

Our job isn't to make standardized tests the center of the universe. It's to make sure our students have the knowledge, skills, and confidence to walk into that testing room, click Begin, and think, "I've got this."

Getting students to that point requires balance. We can't just cross our fingers and hope months of rich, flexible instruction will automatically translate into test-day success. And we can't swing to the other extreme, replacing real, meaningful, rigorous learning with weeks of drill-and-kill test prep that drains all the color from our yellow brick road.

Start with Universal Design and Interleave Standardized Tasks

Preparing students for these tests doesn't mean abandoning universally designed instruction. Instead, we can build a bridge from the learning experiences we design every day to the more rigid structures of standardized measures. The key is to start early, keep the stakes low, and build up gradually.

Begin the year with universally designed assessments that let every student show what they know in ways that work for them. Once students can successfully demonstrate mastery in these flexible environments, introduce a standardized measure as a formative checkpoint and make it clear it's not for a grade. For example, as an English teacher, I might universally design a poetry unit where students explore poems through multiple means of representation. They could listen to audio versions, analyze annotated print copies, and engage in small-group discussions. They'd also have numerous options for sharing their understanding, from writing essays to creating podcasts or visual art.

Once students have successfully analyzed poems in these ways, I'd pause and say something like this: "Now, let's see how you would approach this in a standardized format. This time, you won't have access to the audio or annotated print version, so let's talk about explicit reading strategies and see what you can glean from the text and how you'd answer the multiple-choice questions."

The work can be marked for feedback, but it should not be graded. Afterward, students can reflect on what worked and where they struggled, and they can set personal goals for the next round. Because this strategy gives you regular opportunities to monitor growth, you'll see if certain skills are lagging, and this can help inform targeted interventions. By interleaving standardized mini-tasks about every two weeks, you help students become more comfortable with the format and build strategies for navigating barriers.

Why Interleaving Matters

Interleaving means revisiting skills in different contexts over time rather than teaching one skill in isolation until mastery. It's about mixing skills, returning to them periodically, and giving students multiple chances to apply them under slightly different conditions.

In UDL terms, it's giving students repeated experiences with the supports they need, but it's also helping them practice navigating the barriers they'll face in more standardized measures, gradually building adaptability without overwhelming them. Research shows this approach strengthens retention and helps students adapt to new challenges.[21]

For example, most standardized assessments don't allow tools like speech-to-text or screen readers unless a student has a formal accommodation. As much as we want students to use those supports often, we also want them to feel confident if they don't have them in a particular situation. That's why I advise building a rhythm into the year. On some days, maybe Tech Tuesdays and Thursdays, students have access to every tool in their digital toolbox: speech-to-text, translation, screen readers, annotation tools, you name it. On other days, you may intentionally hold back those supports for short tasks

21 Jonathan Firth et al., "A Systematic Review of Interleaving as a Concept Learning Strategy," *Review of Education* 9, no. 2 (2021): 642–684, https://doi.org/10.7565/ssp.2019.2650.

so students can practice the same skills in a format closer to what they'll encounter on a standardized test, ensuring that students always have access to their formalized accommodations.

This rhythm reduces anxiety when tools aren't available, helps students understand why and when they should use supports, and makes standardized testing conditions feel familiar rather than disruptive.

Universally Design Strategy Instruction Before Practice

As a teacher, I found incredible success introducing standardized mini-tasks every couple of weeks with explicit strategy instruction. For example, you may teach the psychology behind multiple-choice questions, such as how to eliminate distractors or paraphrase questions, and *then* you ask students to tackle a digital passage independently. This mirrors the demands they'll meet later but in a much more accessible way.

One of my favorite teaching moments was challenging students to research how to create high-quality multiple-choice questions. They could work together, use any available resources, and create a booklet, short presentation, video, or written tutorial. Students had the opportunity to explore all the artifacts they made, then choose a challenging text and create a multiple-choice test using what they learned. After this activity, we reviewed previous questions from state standardized tests, not only to answer them but also to try to understand the psychology of the questions. My students' growth scores that year reflected how understanding multiple-choice question design was incredibly helpful for their test-taking strategy tool kit.

This isn't just important for multiple-choice tests. For example, in math, before introducing a no-calculator section, teach or reteach explicit strategies for estimation, mental math, and checking for reasonableness of answers. Offer worked examples, allow students to talk through their process with peers, and give them the chance to apply strategies in small bursts.

By finding a balance between flexible and standardized conditions over the course of the year, students gain two kinds of confidence. First, they'll get reassurance that they can succeed with the supports they know, love, and will have available to them in their lives. Second, they'll feel confident they can navigate the constraints of a standardized assessment because they are capable of doing hard things. These deliberate, spaced opportunities, paired with explicit strategy instruction, help students build both competence and confidence.

Model Strategic Thinking Out Loud

Another super effective strategy, whether students are reading a dense article, solving a multi-step math problem, or analyzing data in science, is to hear an expert (that's you!) think through the process in real time. Before asking students to tackle a task in a standardized format, model your own thought process aloud. Show how you approach a question, how you slow down when you hit a tricky part, and how you check your own reasoning.

In reading, that might mean narrating how you skim the questions first to set a purpose for your reading, then how you annotate the text while ruling out incorrect answer choices. In math, it could mean talking through your approach to a multi-step problem, noting where you might check for reasonableness before committing to an answer. In science, you might verbalize how you extract key data from a graph before reading the accompanying paragraph.

The key is to make the invisible visible to all learners while incorporating UDL principles. When you pair think-alouds with universally designed supports, every learner gains access to the strategies and to your brilliant thinking. Over time, students begin to internalize these metacognitive habits, which help them transfer their learning to high-pressure, standardized conditions.

LEADERSHIP LENS

As leaders, we need to support our educators in finding balance as they design deeper learning experiences that model creativity and innovation while also ensuring that students can transfer what they know to more standardized measures. It's not one or the other. It's both.

This means talking to the educators who consistently have strong outcomes and asking them how they interleave tasks across the year. What do they do in September, October, and January that allows students to feel calm and prepared in May? What rhythms do they build? What feedback structures help students see growth?

It also means talking to students who have experienced incredible growth on standardized measures and asking, "What helped? When did you feel confident? What routines made the unfamiliar feel familiar? What made you believe you could do it?"

As with everything in our schools, this work is about partnership and culture.

Your Move: Integrate a Balance

Think of a lesson you've recently taught or one coming up on your calendar. Now, imagine how you could interleave just one standardized element into that lesson, like a short multiple-choice set, a digital reading passage, or a no-tech problem-solving challenge, but keep the stakes low. Small, intentional changes like these are the bricks that keep your yellow brick road both colorful and connected to the path students will have to travel.

Up Next

We've talked about how to prepare students for standardized tests without sacrificing flexibility, creativity, or preparedness. But even the best-designed lessons and the smartest assessment strategies can't carry the weight of student outcomes alone. For that, we need schoolwide systems that help us remove barriers, share responsibility for learning, and ensure educators have the support to meet every learner's needs. In the next chapter, we'll explore how you can use a multi-tiered system of supports (MTSS) to create the foundation for truly inclusive practice—so that what you design in your classroom is backed up by the structures around you.

CHAPTER 9

Systems That Support Flexibility

The Question That Changed the Room

Recently, I was facilitating a professional development session on UDL for a district, and the teachers were all in. You could feel the energy in the room. Educators were nodding, jotting down notes, turning to neighbors with that *oh, I could try this tomorrow* look. But as soon as we got to the Q&A, one teacher posed the million-dollar question: "This all makes sense . . . but what happens when the system we work in isn't set up for this?"

This question is not unique. It highlights why so many educators love the idea of UDL but struggle to put it into practice. It's not because they don't believe in it. It's because the system wasn't built for this level of innovation, inclusion, and collaboration. That's exactly why we need to talk about building a multi-tiered system of supports, which, in my view, is the best darn framework to support teachers without expecting them to shoulder it all alone.

Why Systems Matter for UDL

Designing flexible lessons is a powerful start, but it's only part of the equation. To truly reach every learner, we also need systems to support that flexibility. I'm sure you recognize that the students you serve are becoming increasingly diverse—and not just in ways that are formally documented. Often, when we talk about inclusion, the conversation centers on students with IEPs or 504 plans. But our classrooms and schools are far more complex than that. We are working to support multilingual learners, students navigating mental health challenges, students experiencing poverty, students managing trauma, and students who need significant acceleration and enrichment. That's a lot. It's a lot to expect teachers to meet all those needs with a handful of strategies or a one-time PD session.

If the broader system isn't built to support flexibility, if educators are stretched thin, if supports are inconsistent, if inclusion is treated like a checkbox, we will keep running into the same walls. The promise of UDL can't be fulfilled in classrooms alone; it has to be matched by schoolwide structures grounded in equity, access, and high expectations.

Defining Inclusion vs. Inclusive Practice

Inclusion and *inclusive practice* are often used interchangeably, but they are not the same thing. Inclusion is a critical first step because it ensures that students with support needs are physically present in classrooms with their peers. But presence alone doesn't guarantee access; there is nothing magical about moving a student's seat into a different room. That's where inclusive practice comes in. It means designing instruction so that all students, regardless of their variability, can access rigorous grade-level content, feel supported, and be challenged in meaningful ways. Inclusive practice requires systems that give teachers time, tools, and collaboration to design learning for the students they actually serve, not the "average" student, who doesn't exist.

This isn't just a philosophical shift. These ideas are also at the center of current debates in the field. I recently read about Professor Doug Fuchs's examination of the research on inclusion in the Hechinger Report,[22] and he argued that the evidence for special education inclusion is "fundamentally flawed."

Too often, inclusion is implemented without a flexible curriculum, robust scaffolding, adequate teacher preparation, or collaboration with related service providers. Without these conditions, the general education classroom can feel overwhelming for both students and teachers. While Fuchs's critique initially prompted some defensiveness, the more I reflected, the more I realized that our field must double down on the work ahead, moving beyond merely placing students in general education settings to constructing a comprehensive, responsive instructional system that meets the needs of all educators and students.

The Hechinger Report included a compelling observation:

> Clearly, a good version of inclusion will outperform a bad version of a separate classroom. And a good version of intense, specialized instruction will outperform a bad version of an inclusive classroom where the general education teacher is overwhelmed and lacks training. Too often, students aren't getting the support they need.[23]

This statement resonates deeply with me. As a lifelong educator and a mom of four, one of whom has support needs, I believe

22 Jill Barshay, "Top Scholar Says Evidence for Special-Education Inclusion Is 'Fundamentally Flawed,'" Hechinger Report, January 13, 2025, https://hechingerreport.org/proof-points-special-education-inclusion-research-flawed/.

23 Barshay, "Top Scholar."

it with my whole heart. It reminds us that the promise of inclusion is only fulfilled when schools invest in the conditions necessary for high-quality implementation. For all students to succeed, every teacher must be set up for success, too.

What High-Quality Inclusion Looks Like

Let's talk about what that actually looks like in practice. It means ensuring that students who need speech-language services or behavior support don't have to miss core instruction to receive them. It means co-teaching models that go beyond "you teach, I'll help" to true shared ownership of the classroom. It means providing enough staff so students can receive what they need without being pulled out of grade-level instruction with subject matter experts or missing opportunities to collaborate with peers. It means giving teachers enough time to plan *together*, problem-solve, adjust, and align their work with grade-level expectations and learner variability.

This work also requires clarity about roles. Too often, the responsibility for inclusion rests entirely on general educators who lack adequate training or support. In a well-designed system, inclusive education is a shared responsibility. General education teachers bring expertise in curriculum and instruction. Special educators and support providers bring deep knowledge of accommodations, modifications, and specialized strategies. And when we create space for those roles to work together, we get far better outcomes for students. All of this requires time to plan, reflect, and adjust together, and the system must make that time possible.

Enter MTSS

When we talk about MTSS, it's easy to picture a triangle (see figure 9.1) or think of it as another layer of educational jargon. But at its heart, MTSS is a system built to help you do what you already do best: meet students where they are and help them grow.

A multi-tiered system of supports ensures that every student receives what they need to succeed academically, socially, emotionally, and behaviorally while continuing to have access to first and best instruction with their peers. The *MT* recognizes that some students need added support in addition to rigorous Tier 1. The *SS* ensures educators have the time, tools, and structures to deliver that support well. It is not just a framework for interventions; it's a framework for teaching and learning. It begins with two beliefs. The first is that all students can learn at high levels when given access to strong, inclusive instruction. The second is that educators can do this work when given appropriate leadership, system support, professional development, and resources.

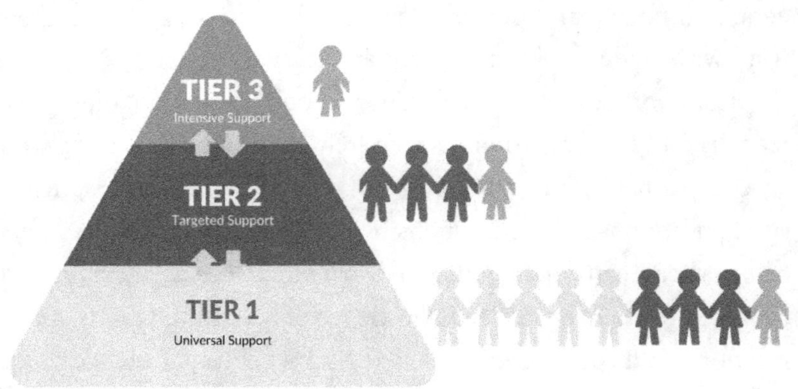

Figure 9.1: Three Tiers of Instruction

Tier 1: The Foundation

MTSS begins with Tier 1, the first and best instruction all students receive. When Tier 1 instruction is robust, engaging, and universally designed, most students thrive without needing additional interventions. Implementation research and expert consensus in MTSS frameworks suggest that effective Tier 1 instruction can meet the needs of approximately 80 percent of students.[24] So when the core isn't meeting students' needs, it's not a signal to start creating more small groups or pulling students out; it's a signal to strengthen the foundation. We can't intervene our way out of weak Tier 1 instruction, but we also can't wish our way out. We need real system support to make the instructional shifts that align to UDL, data-based decision-making, and collaboration.

Tier 2: The Some

Once Tier 1 is strong, we can layer in Tier 2, which provides targeted, supplemental instruction or interventions for students who need more than Tier 1. Tier 2 support is in addition to, not instead of, core instruction, and it's often given in small groups and focused on specific skills or gaps. If data shows that a group of students needs explicit work on a reading comprehension strategy, math concept, or self-regulation skill, we zoom in without removing them from the rigor and flexibility of the Tier 1 experience.

Sometimes students are pulled out of Tier 1 because the schedule, staffing, or co-planning structures don't allow push-in support to work well. That is not a teacher problem; it is a system-design problem. It may feel like these structures are out of your control, but your insight matters. Start the conversation that leads to change by saying, "To truly support our students, here is what we need." This is professional advocacy, not complaining. Tier 2 must be built into the system, not solved individually in isolated classrooms. That means protected intervention time, co-planning structures, and staffing models where push-in is the default, not the exception.

24 Institute of Education Sciences, "Key Terms Handout." *Regional Educational Laboratory Appalachia,* January 2025, https://ies.ed.gov/rel-appalachia/2025/01/key-terms-handout.

Tier 3: The Few

Tier 3 provides the most intensive, individualized support. It does not replace participation in Tier 1, nor is it synonymous with special education. It supplements core instruction with highly focused, personalized teaching, often daily and sometimes coordinated with additional services.

Some people may ask, "What if our school is a specialized program and we're already Tier 3?" I'd still challenge you to consider what you offer to all your learners in terms of academic, behavioral, and social-emotional instruction as well as targeted and individualized support. Consider the foundation of your site. As our districts become more inclusive, we hope to minimize the need for separate programs and settings to provide all students with the programming they need.

The SS: The System of Supports

When MTSS is implemented well, movement between tiers is fluid. Students get what they need, when they need it, without losing access to inclusion, belonging, and grade-level learning. This is where the system of supports matters most.

Consider figure 9.2, which shows the support system surrounding the multiple tiers. In their landmark implementation science study, researchers from the National Implementation Research Network linked strong system supports with increased student outcomes.[25] Based on this research, effective multi-tiered systems cannot rely on interventions alone; they require intentional, aligned system supports that build adult capacity, ensure fidelity, and sustain implementation over time.

25 Karen A. Blase et al., "Implementation Science: Changing Hearts, Minds, Behavior, and Systems to Improve Educational Outcomes," National Implementation Research Network, Frank Porter Graham Child Development Institute, University of North Carolina at Chapel Hill, 2015, 17.

The drivers, or the cogs of the system, are the system conditions that make evidence-based inclusive instruction possible. They are not "extras." They are the infrastructure that allows educators to design, teach, reflect, and improve. When these drivers are in place, MTSS becomes doable, sustainable, and effective. When they are missing, we end up relying on individual heroics.

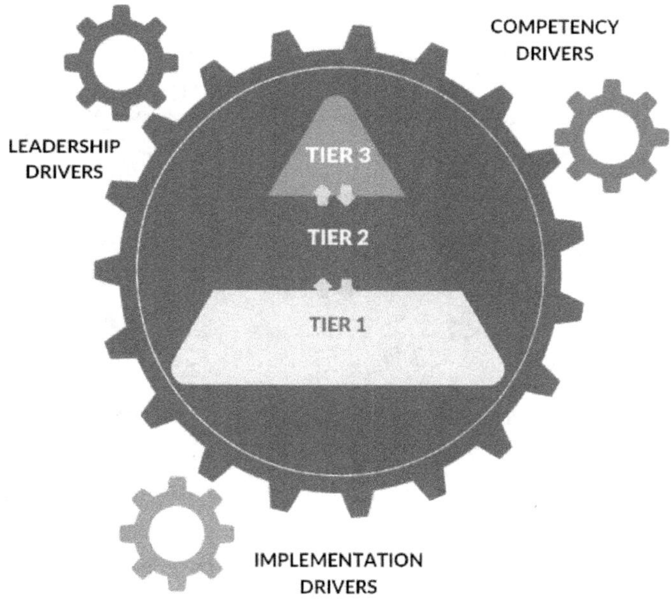

Figure 9.2: System of Support

Leadership Drivers

First, let's examine the leadership drivers. These are how the system is guided, protected, and sustained. Leaders set the conditions that make implementation possible, not by doing all the work but by removing barriers and reinforcing priorities. Leaders need to create a culture and climate to better meet the needs of all learners, allocate resources to ensure adequate staffing models and schedules, protect instructional time, create space for professional learning, and help to engage families and community partners to develop a comprehensive educational experience that honors students and everyone who serves them.

And if you're reading this as a classroom teacher, you play a critical role in this work. You can be part of a distributed leadership team, share what you're noticing with colleagues and leaders, and ask to take part in shaping a clear instructional vision for your school. You can bring forward examples of strong student work, patterns you're seeing in learning needs, and ideas for how schedules or collaboration time could better support instruction.

Leadership is not about directing teachers; it is about building the conditions where teachers can do their best work. If you're in the classroom, surface what is working, what is getting in the way, and which specific conditions would help your students most.

LEADERSHIP LENS

Strong leadership is essential for setting the vision for MTSS and ensuring implementation integrity as we work toward including all learners while increasing their outcomes. MTSS doesn't work because we talk about inclusion and deeper learning. It works because leaders systematically create the conditions that allow inclusive practices to thrive.

As a leader, you must be committed to the following:

- **Engaging in data-driven decision-making and continuous improvement.** This is about more than collecting data. It's about ensuring that educators have the skill set and resources to use the data to drive instructional shifts, reflect on what's working, and adjust supports before small gaps widen.
- **Building the skills and knowledge of educators to implement MTSS effectively.** This includes protecting time for collaboration, encouraging shared problem-solving, and fostering a culture where educators learn from one another.

- **Providing sustained professional development and ongoing coaching.** One-and-done workshops do not lead to change. MTSS grows when teachers receive modeling, feedback, and time to practice new approaches over time.

When leaders prioritize these commitments, MTSS becomes a true system of support, not a compliance requirement. This shift is necessary if we're going to move from the systems we have to the ones that better serve students, educators, and families. Use this lens to advocate for the time, tools, and collaboration your students need.

Competency Drivers

Now that we've looked at leadership drivers, we'll talk about competency drivers, which focus on building the skills, confidence, and collective efficacy of the adults in the system. This is where your day-to-day work as an educator is supported and strengthened. Competency drivers include ongoing professional development, instructional coaching, PLCs, mentoring, reflection cycles, and opportunities to observe and learn from colleagues. When schools invest in these, teachers do not have to reinvent everything from scratch or rely solely on trial and error. Educators learn together, share strategies, and refine practices based on evidence of what works for students. Research funded by the US Department of Education shows that teachers who engage in sustained professional learning for up to forty-nine hours a year see significant gains in student outcomes.[26]

If your school does not yet have embedded structures for this, start where you can: Request collaborative planning time, instructional rounds, resource support, or PD in a focused area. You can say, "I know we're working to create inclusive classrooms, and I want

26 Kwang Suk Yoon et al., *Reviewing the Evidence on How Teacher Professional Development Affects Student Achievement*, Issues & Answers Report, REL 2007, no. 033, US Department of Education, Institute of Education Sciences, National Center for Education Evaluation and Regional Assistance (2007).

to get better at it. I am not feeling fully prepared yet, and I would love to learn more about . . ." The goal is progress, not perfection, and we are better when we put our skill sets together.

Implementation Drivers

Finally, the implementation drivers are the nuts and bolts that determine whether inclusive practices can actually be used in real classrooms. These drivers include access to high-quality instructional materials, reliable technology, and authentic and meaningful data, along with practices that ensure we have systems in place to know what's working and what isn't yet. That way, we can put our brilliant heads together to address any barriers or problems of practice. Implementation drivers are often invisible when they're working well and painfully obvious when they're not. As an educator, you can play a powerful role here by naming what's getting in the way, e.g., "We don't have access to the technology that would allow this student to thrive" or "We need materials that better support multilingual learners." Then you can also propose what would make the biggest difference.

You now have the pieces: strong Tier 1 for all, responsive Tier 2 and Tier 3, and drivers that make the work possible. The next step is alignment. This starts with a clear instructional vision that everyone can point to when making decisions about time, support, and resources.

Your Move: Start with Instructional Vision

Before a school can build a system that truly works for all learners, it needs a shared instructional vision. Without this clear picture of great instruction, even strong efforts feel scattered. You might have excellent individual lessons, creative interventions, and dedicated teachers, but if everyone is aiming at a slightly different picture of "great instruction," it's hard to build a system that helps all students succeed.

An instructional vision is a clear, shared understanding of what high-quality teaching and learning look like in practice. It's not a poster in the hallway or a paragraph in a strategic plan; it's something that shapes daily decisions about instruction, support, and time. When a vision is clear, it guides everything else: how teachers plan lessons, how teams use data, how interventions are scheduled, and how resources are allocated. When it's missing, the system struggles to stay aligned.

As an educator, you have an essential role in shaping and advocating for that vision. You see every day what works for students and where the system falls short. You know what equitable, inclusive teaching looks like in real classrooms. If your school doesn't yet have a shared instructional vision, you can start the conversation. In a PLC, staff meeting, or professional learning session, you might say, "We all want students to feel successful here. What does great instruction look like for us? How can we describe that so it becomes our collective goal?"

Here are a few prompts you can use to start the conversation with colleagues:

- What do we believe students should experience every day in our classrooms?
- How do we define great teaching in our school or district?
- How do we ensure that all students, including multilingual learners, students with disabilities, and students who need enrichment, can access grade-level learning?
- How do we measure success in ways that go beyond test scores?

Once you have some shared answers, connect them to MTSS. A strong instructional vision is the anchor for Tier 1—the "all." It defines what core instruction should look like when it's universally designed to anticipate barriers and include all learners. It also guides how you identify and deliver support in Tiers 2 and 3. When the vision is clear, interventions align with core instruction instead of replacing it, and all staff work from the same understanding of what students are striving toward.

You can use the instructional vision to advocate for what teachers and students need. When schedules, staffing, or PD are discussed, connect your ideas back to the vision. Here are some examples:

- "Our vision emphasizes co-planning and inclusive Tier 1 instruction. We need protected time to plan together."
- "Our vision commits to keeping all students in grade-level work. We need to coordinate interventions so students don't miss core instruction."
- "Our vision centers on student agency and belonging. We need ongoing professional learning in UDL and restorative practices."

When you frame your advocacy around the shared vision, your voice carries more weight. You're not asking for personal preferences. You're reinforcing what the system says it values.

If your school already has a vision statement, take a closer look at it. Does it actually describe what great teaching and learning look like in your classroom? Does it reflect the principles of UDL and MTSS? If it feels outdated or vague, invite your team to revisit it. Ask, "Does this still represent the way we want students to experience learning here?" When you speak up about what great instruction should look like for *all* students and what systems are needed to support it, you're shaping the foundation of MTSS and modeling what inclusive leadership looks like.

To learn more about the MTSS drivers and how they serve a clear instructional vision, explore the MTSS self-assessment linked to the QR code at the beginning of the book. This tool, adapted from the MTSS Self-Assessment tool in my book *In Support of Students* (co-authored with my colleague Kristan Rodriguez), helps you identify what will scale your UDL work now and what should move into future strategic planning. Remember that all learners can be successful when we get the conditions right. Building a multi-tiered system of supports ensures educators have the support and conditions to serve the brilliant students in our schools today.

Up Next

The final chapter is your bridge from reflection to action. So, take a deep breath, grab your metaphorical dance shoes, and get ready to step onto the floor one more time. You've got the knowledge, the mindset, and the heart. Now it's time to make this shift your own.

PART 4

Putting It All Together

CHAPTER 10

You've Got This. Really.

The End of the Road

If I'm being honest, writing this last chapter feels a little like the end of a middle school dance. Back then, they always wrapped up with "End of the Road" by Boyz II Men, and no matter how much fun you'd had, you'd feel that little wave of sadness because you knew it was almost over. Well, friends, here we are—the last few minutes on the dance floor. But unlike those dances, this is not the end. This is the part where you take everything we've explored together and make it yours.

We've tackled the big ideas and the practical moves: dismantling one-size-fits-all instruction, making peace with standardized testing, and building the multi-tiered systems that ensure teachers aren't left to do it all alone. But now it comes down to this: What happens when you step back into your own classroom, office, or meeting room? The message here is honor yourselves and take it slow.

I say this because I *love* teachers. Over the years, I've been lucky enough to work with teachers all over the world, and here's what I know: You show up for kids. Every single day. You rally when there's a crisis. You're in the stands at games. You collect winter coats. You make sure students know there's an adult who will always be in their corner. That's why I believe so strongly in your capacity to do this work—not because it's easy but because you already do the hard stuff every day.

And yet, here's the truth: A lot of the practices we've relied on for decades weren't designed with all kids in mind, especially not the kids we serve today. They're growing up in a world of instant information, personalized playlists, and on-demand everything (can you imagine if we'd been able to DoorDash our lunches in high school?). They don't just want options; they expect them. And when learning doesn't reflect that reality, it can create barriers before we've even started. So, there's a lot we need to adjust, but it doesn't have to happen all at once. Rather, think about how you can take what you've learned throughout this book and apply it to your own unique learning environment to honor firm goals and flexible means.

One tool that may be helpful as you take these next steps is the UDL Lesson Planning Protocol, a tool that I created in partnership with my incredible team of consultants. Please know that it's not another "you must do it this way" mandate. It's a flexible, step-by-step companion you can adapt to your context, time, and resources. The goal is to make your planning process more intentional and more inclusive.

This protocol can be the bridge between what you've learned and what you'll do next. Every step is rooted in the tenets we've talked about since chapter 1: anticipating variability, designing with firm goals and flexible means, and creating opportunities for students to own their learning. It's also built with the realities of teaching in mind: limited time, diverse needs, and the ongoing balance between individual creativity and systemic alignment. Think of it as the playlist for your next "dance." You already know the songs. You've practiced the moves. Now you get to decide the order, the tempo, and the style that will make it yours, 4 percent at a time!

Planning with Purpose: Tips for Using This Protocol

While the UDL Lesson Planning Protocol is designed with K–12 classrooms in mind, the same process can be used when designing professional learning, coaching sessions, or adult education experiences. Just like in K–12 settings, adult learners benefit from clear goals, flexible methods, opportunities for voice and choice, and a strong sense of belonging. Whether you're planning a PD session, a team meeting, or a coaching cycle, these steps support intentional, inclusive design for all learners. We use the term *students* throughout this tool, but the steps apply equally when working with educators, families, or community members. Feel free to adapt the language to fit your context. But first, let's examine a few tips!

- **Stay student centered.** Keep the focus on creating learning experiences that support access, engagement, and demonstrated growth for every student. Revisit the goal often and check whether design choices are responsive to learner variability.
- **Reflect with purpose.** Use the guiding questions in each step to make intentional decisions about design. Reflecting on student experience and variability helps you identify barriers and consider flexible strategies to reduce them.
- **Collaborate with colleagues.** Use the protocol in team planning to share insights, align practices, and expand ideas for supporting diverse learners. Collaboration strengthens capacity to design more fully inclusive learning environments.

- **Use AI to support your thinking.** Each step includes an optional prompt that can be used with generative AI tools. These prompts can help you brainstorm ideas, develop scaffolds, and explore flexible options. AI should be used to enhance your expertise and decision-making, not replace it.
- **Use it to refine, not redo.** This protocol is not about starting from scratch. It's a flexible planning companion that helps you sharpen and build on what you already do, especially when time is tight in our increasingly complex learning environments.
- **Start small.** Choose one step to focus on when planning or revising a learning experience. While beginning with a single step may not fully eliminate all access barriers, it provides a practical and strategic entry point for building fluency with universally designed instruction.

Now, let's dive into the process. As you reflect on these tips, consider how they align to your current practice, how you could continue to grow, and what system shifts would support you as you transition to more universally designed planning.

Step 1: Clarify the Purpose

Guiding questions:

- What is the clear, grade-level standard or learning objective for this learning experience?
- Why is this learning important, and how will it be useful to students now and in the future?
- How will students have opportunities to set goals to own and increase their learning?

Why it matters: Begin by analyzing the standard or learning goal, then break it into precise, student-friendly learning targets that make expectations explicit and accessible. A clear, grade-level-aligned goal communicated to students sets the foundation for purposeful, inclusive instruction. When students can articulate the learning goal and its relevance, they are more likely to engage meaningfully, persist through rigorous tasks, and demonstrate mastery.

AI prompt: I'm teaching [standard] to [grade]. Break this into clear, student-friendly objectives I can share with learners. Include success criteria to help students track their progress. Explain why this learning matters and suggest ways students can set personal goals as they work toward the objective.

Step 2: Anticipate Variability

Guiding questions:

- What prior knowledge or misconceptions may affect learning?
- What barriers (academic, social, sensory, or behavioral) might impact student engagement or success?
- What supports or scaffolds will be necessary to eliminate these barriers and ensure all students can meet the goal?
- What extensions or opportunities for deeper learning will be necessary to challenge students who are ready for more?

Why it matters: Learner variability is natural and expected. It's not just about how students differ from one another but also how the same student might engage differently from day to day. Emotions, focus, lived experience, prior knowledge, and language all influence how students interact with content and with others. Use classroom data or team insights such as formative assessments, IEP goals, screeners, or behavioral observations to predict barriers and identify proactive supports. When we anticipate variability, we can design standards-aligned lessons that maintain firm goals while incorporating instructional flexibility grounded in UDL principles. This allows all students to access learning and show what they know.

AI prompt: What are common misconceptions and predictable barriers in [standard] for [grade]? Generate scaffolds to reduce these barriers and suggest extensions for students who are ready for deeper learning.

Step 3: Build a Welcoming Start

Guiding questions:

- How will I welcome students and create a sense of belonging in the learning environment?
- How will I establish an inclusive and academically supportive space that invites participation and encourages risk-taking?
- How will I activate or connect to students' background knowledge and prior experiences to spark interest in the learning?

Why it matters: A welcoming start establishes a predictable, inclusive environment that fosters academic risk-taking and sets the tone for high-level learning. When routines build a sense of belonging and students are invited to connect to prior knowledge or personal relevance, they are more likely to engage meaningfully and persist through challenging tasks.

AI prompt: Suggest a universally designed opener for [standard] in [grade] that builds a welcoming tone, fosters a sense of belonging, encourages active participation, and activates background knowledge to support engagement with the learning objective.

Step 4: Design Flexible Assessments

Guiding questions:

- How will students show what they know and can do?
- What success criteria or rubrics will support clarity and self-assessment?
- How will I provide timely, meaningful feedback throughout the learning process?

Why it matters: When students have multiple ways to demonstrate their learning, they are more likely to engage meaningfully, and they are better able to demonstrate standards-based understanding in ways that align with their strengths. Clear success criteria and flexible assessment options support student agency, deepen metacognition, and allow all students to reflect on progress, not just performance.

AI prompt: Suggest three assessment options for [standard] in [grade] that provide student choice. Create a rubric with descriptions of progressing in, meeting, and exceeding expectations.

Step 5: Design Flexible Learning Experiences

Guiding questions:

- How will students access and process the learning in ways that reflect their strengths and needs?

- How will students deepen their understanding through interactions with ideas, tasks, and tools?
- What flexible options (e.g., working individually, in pairs, or in small groups) will help all students stay engaged in learning and help them progress toward the goal?

Why it matters: Once the learning objective and success criteria are clear, variability is anticipated, students are welcomed into the learning space, and you've considered how you will measure learning through construct-relevant assessments, the next step is to design experiences that support how students learn. Instruction that incorporates active engagement supports deeper understanding, especially when students have flexible options for accessing and exploring content. When learning is intentionally designed with flexibility, students are more likely to access complex ideas, persist through challenges, and build the knowledge and skills needed to meet the learning objective.

AI prompt: How can I design a lesson for [standard] at [grade] so that students are not expected to learn in the same way? What are flexible ways students can access and process the learning? How can I leverage small-group instruction as one of several options for support?

Step 6: Create Space for Student Ownership

Guiding questions:

- How will students reflect on their learning and set goals for improvement?
- How will I invite student questions, feedback, and co-creation?

- How will students monitor their own growth over time?

Why it matters: Deep learning occurs when students can reflect on their progress, assess their strategies, and adjust their approach to meet goals. Opportunities for reflection, feedback, and self-monitoring build ownership, agency, and motivation. When students have a voice in the learning process, they are more likely to stay engaged and take initiative.

AI prompt: Suggest simple reflection prompts or tools for students in [grade] to track their progress on [standard]. How can I invite students to give feedback and contribute to shaping the learning experience?

Step 7: Plan an Intentional Close

Guiding questions:

- How will I summarize and celebrate student learning?
- How will I support emotional closure or reset before transitioning?
- What routines will reinforce relationships and readiness for what's next?

Why it matters: A strong close to a lesson, unit, or learning experience reinforces mastery, highlights key takeaways, and creates space for students to reflect on their learning. Purposeful closing routines reinforce key concepts, promote reflection, and signal the value of the learning process.

AI prompt: What are simple, inclusive routines to end a lesson/unit on [standard] for [grade] that support emotional regulation, reinforce community, and help students reflect on their learning?

Your Move: From Reading to Doing

Choose a lesson you'll teach (or a meeting you'll lead) in the next two weeks. Use the UDL Lesson Planning Protocol and walk through each step, making intentional choices to anticipate variability, build belonging, and create space for ownership.

Then, once you design a learning opportunity and facilitate it, go back to your most important audience, your learners, and ask them how it went. What helped them learn? What got in the way? What would they change? Their feedback is your next set of design notes because the real magic isn't in getting it "right" the first time. It's in refining, adapting, and growing together. As I've said, we can all experience success when the conditions are right, and our learners are in a great place to help us figure out exactly what those conditions are. So, onward!

Up Next

The last song might be playing, but your dance is just getting started. You've got this. Really.

Acknowledgments

This book would not exist without you, my incredible, brilliant, hilarious colleagues at Novak Education. You help me keep it real, push my thinking, and, continually grow my skills as both an educator and a leader. Truly, you are the best professional learning network I could ever imagine. I am *so* grateful for each of you and for your commitment to educators and the learners they serve. Somewhere along the way, we also became dear friends, which is one of the most beautiful gifts of this work. And the laughs. Goodness, how you all bring me joy. Thank you from the bottom of my heart. I can't wait until the next retreat.

David Gordon, my UDL-Pawtucket brother, I am so grateful to you for supporting this book through the developmental editing stage. There is truly no one better suited to provide feedback on a book about UDL, and I feel incredibly lucky that you were available as a freelancer and that George and Paige were open to having you support this work. #UDLforlife. This book is so much stronger because of you. We must celebrate over pancakes at the Friendly Toast!

George, thank you, always. You are the older brother I always wanted, an amazing friend, and a pain in the neck in exactly the right ways. When I said, "I think I have an idea for a book," you were all in, as you always are. I love you for that! Paige, thank you for putting up with both me and George. (: You absolutely have your work cut out for you, and you meet it with grace, positivity, and responsiveness every single time.

And Lon. You do the heavy lifting every single day. You chauffeur our kids (thank goodness Torin finally got his license!), take care of the house (and the lawn, of course), and create the space that allows me to focus on being a mom, a teacher, a runner, and a writer. Oh, and the best wife ever! As my mom always says about my dad, and as I say about you, you were the best decision I have ever made. If I could go back, I would not change a thing. Well, except maybe *White Heat*. I love you always.

About Katie Novak

Katie Novak, Ed.D., is a nationally recognized leader in inclusive education and school improvement. With twenty-five years of experience in education and a background as a classroom teacher, curriculum coordinator, and assistant superintendent, she brings deep practical expertise and real-world perspective to her work.

Katie is widely known for translating complex frameworks like Universal Design for Learning (UDL), multi-tiered systems of supports (MTSS), and inclusive practices into clear, actionable strategies that educators can actually use. Her work helps schools move beyond compliance toward instruction that is rigorous, engaging, and responsive to learner variability.

An instructor at the University of Pennsylvania and the author of seventeen books, including this one, with more than 350,000 copies sold worldwide, Katie doesn't just write about change—she leads it. Through consulting, professional learning, and systems-level coaching, she partners with districts to design professional development that sticks and instructional practices that last.

Known for blending research, clarity, and warmth, Katie brings both evidence and humanity to her work. Whether she's supporting district leaders, facilitating learning with educators, or training for a fifty-mile race, she approaches everything with purpose, heart, and a deep belief that better is always possible.

More from IMPRESS

ImpressBooks.org

Empower: What Happens When Students Own Their Learning by A.J. Juliani and John Spencer

Learner-Centered Innovation: Spark Curiosity, Ignite Passion, and Unleash Genius by Katie Martin

Unleash Talent: Bringing Out the Best in Yourself and the Learners You Serve by Kara Knollmeyer

Reclaiming Our Calling: Hold On to the Heart, Mind, and Hope of Education by Brad Gustafson

Take the L.E.A.P.: Ignite a Culture of Innovation by Elisabeth Bostwick

Drawn to Teach: An Illustrated Guide to Transforming Your Teaching written by Josh Stumpenhorst and illustrated by Trevor Guthke

Math Recess: Playful Learning in an Age of Disruption by Sunil Singh and Dr. Christopher Brownell

Innovate inside the Box: Empowering Learners Through UDL and Innovator's Mindset by George Couros and Katie Novak

Personal & Authentic: Designing Learning Experiences That Last a Lifetime by Thomas C. Murray

Learner-Centered Leadership: A Blueprint for Transformational Change in Learning Communities by Devin Vodicka

Kids These Days: A Game Plan for (Re)Connecting with Those We Teach, Lead & Love by Dr. Jody Carrington

UDL and Blended Learning: Thriving in Flexible Learning Landscapes by Katie Novak and Catlin Tucker

Teachers These Days: Stories & Strategies for Reconnection by Dr. Jody Carrington and Laurie McIntosh

Because of a Teacher: Stories of the Past to Inspire the Future of Education written and curated by George Couros

Because of a Teacher, Volume 2: Stories from the First Years of Teaching written and curated by George Couros

Evolving Education: Shifting to a Learner-Centered Paradigm by Katie Martin

Adaptable: How to Create an Adaptable Curriculum and Flexible Learning Experiences That Work in Any Environment by A.J. Juliani

Lead from Where You Are: Building Intention, Connection, and Direction in Our Schools by Joe Sanfelippo

The Shift to Student-Led: Reimagining Classroom Workflows with UDL and Blended Learning by Catlin R. Tucker and Katie Novak

The Design Thinking Classroom: Using Design Thinking to Reimagine the Role and Practice of Educators by David Jakes

Shift Writing into the Classroom with UDL and Blended Learning by Catlin R. Tucker and Katie Novak

Teach Happy: Small Steps to Big Joy by Kim Strobel

What Makes a Great Principal by George Couros and Allyson Apsey

Hopes for School: A Student's Experience and Ideas for Educational Transformation by Karen Phan and Jennifer Casa-Todd

Elevating Educational Design with AI: Making Learning Accessible, Inclusive, and Equitable by Catlin R. Tucker and Katie Novak

The Station Rotation Model & UDL: Elevate Tier 1 Instruction and Cultivate Learner Agency by Catlin R. Tucker

Forward, Together by George Couros

www.ingramcontent.com/pod-product-compliance
Lightning Source LLC
LaVergne TN
LVHW020046110826
845155LV00029B/648

* 9 7 8 1 9 4 8 3 3 4 8 5 3 *